WHEN THOUGHT
TURNS TO LIGHT

When Thought Turns to Light

A Practical Guide to Spiritual Transformation

Patrick Paul Garlinger

Epigraph Books
Rhinebeck, New York

Paperback ISBN: 978-1-944037-47-5
E-book ISBN: 978-1-944037-48-2
Library of Congress Control Number: 2016955898

Cover design by Colin Rolfe
Interior design by Colin Rolfe

Epigraph Books
22 East Market Street, Suite 304
Rhinebeck, NY 12572
(845) 876-4861
www.epigraphps.com

For Max,
Mirabai,
the Divine Mothers,
and my Mother,
with endless gratitude for teaching me to
open my heart more than I ever thought was possible.

Contents

Part I: Awakening

Part II: Transformation

PART I
AWAKENING

Chapter 1

Light: We Are Energy

When you surrender and let go,
the Light comes into you,
because the Light is you.
— Mirabai Devi, *Samadhi*

HAVE YOU EVER FELT SUCH PURE and unconditional love from another human being that you were brought to tears? Our first taste of unconditional love often comes from a parent or grandparent, and then ideally from a life partner. Many of us feel unconditional love for our children or pets, but most of our relationships are not perfect examples of unconditional love. Our attitudes toward each other are often punctuated by annoyance, frustration, or disappointment when our expectations are not met, making the love we give and receive very much conditional.

While our experience of unconditional love is sporadic at best, there are some for whom unconditional love is a natural state of being. These are known as Avatars or *satgurus* (the Sanskrit term for "true master"), and are sometimes referred to as Ascended Masters once they have passed out of this life. They come into this world knowing fully and completely how divine we all truly are. Avatars are enlightened, filled with love, and devoted exclusively to helping us embrace our divine nature. Jesus Christ was certainly the most well-known and misunderstood Avatar of the last two millennia. There are many who have followed, such as Sai Baba, and some who are alive today, such as Amma, Mother Meera, and Karunamayi.

The first time I saw Amma, a diminutive Indian woman, she radiated more love than I have ever felt from another human being. My eyes moistened with tears as I felt waves of love pouring out of her; I had never seen her before, yet it felt like I had always known her.

Amma hugs people. When she hugs you, it's called *darshan*, which is the Sanskrit term for "vision of God." It is essentially a transfer of energy. She holds you closely for about fifteen seconds, and during that time she transmits energy into you. It's brief but incredibly powerful. My first hug was so intense that I began heaving and choking on tears as an immense amount of sorrow came up, as if something heavy and burdensome were being lifted and replaced by utter bliss. I remember thinking, as tears rolled down my face, *How can I be crying? I just met this person!* Afterwards I sat for some time, completely filled with feelings of love and peace.

Mother Meera, another Avatar, explains that when she gives darshan, "I am giving Light to every part of your being; I am opening every part of you to the Light."[1] During darshan, the Avatar transmits her energy directly into you, thereby allowing you to experience a much higher frequency of energy than you are accustomed to. That energy—what Mother Meera calls "Light"—is the feeling of pure, unconditional love.

Avatars are not the only ones who are directly connected to the Light. In December 2010, several months prior to my encounter with Amma, I met Mirabai Devi, whose gift was described as the ability to transmit "Light" into others. I was intrigued, but had no expectations; I did not consider myself to be a religious person, so some part of me didn't believe that I would feel any sort of energy.

What I experienced was beyond words. When Mirabai began her transmission of Light, I felt an intense energy immediately begin to stream into my head, through the space between my eyebrows, which I later learned is the "third eye." The energy felt like an immense, golden light, and afterwards I felt that I was filled with a tremendous glow. I had never experienced anything like it. It was better than sex, drugs, or alcohol, for sure. It felt like I was wrapped in a perfect blanket of love and bliss.

Although I did not know it at the time, my encounters with Mirabai and Amma marked a watershed in my own transformation. They taught me that our human potential is so much greater than we think. All of us are connected to the same Light, because that connection is inherent in being alive. The Light—the energy of unconditional love—flows through all of us. We are always connected to the Light, and we are all capable of feeling and expressing unconditional love.

Words

When I first began to experience the Light, I thought to myself, *God exists!* That was not a word that I had used often, and I had been reluctant to probe deeply into the question of whether God existed. As a logic-based person, I generally thought of God as a human construct that reflected a deep-seated need for something larger than one's self. But, if pressed, I would have been willing to say that I was open to evidence of God's existence, as if giving myself an out just in case there *was* a God.

At some point in life, everyone asks if God exists. Yet there is probably no question more divisive than the existence of a higher power. Part of the problem lies within the word itself. John the Apostle wrote in the Bible, "In the beginning was the Word, and the Word was God," but ever since then, we have been stuck at the beginning, hung up on the very word *God*. As the well-known spiritual teacher Eckhart Tolle has suggested, we might as well drop the word altogether; for too many people, *God* calls to mind a white-bearded man meting out punishment with a thunderbolt, and invokes a religious history that immediately raises people's hackles.

Why not simply choose another word? We could use *Infinite*, *Spirit*, or *Source*, although these words carry a certain New Age connotation that some may find offensive. We could also use the words *Life*, *Universe*, *Being*, or *Now* to avoid any religious or spiritual connotations. We could just as well use the word *Love*.

As Tolle reminds us, all of these are efforts to capture in a single word something that is actually beyond all language. No single word is going to be adequate. Each word we use will carry with it some sort of historical baggage, or some piece of an old paradigm or belief system. That paradigm or belief system will limit one's ability to come to a new understanding of the source of energy that is in all life. Words like *God* and *Divine* cast a long shadow over any other word that might be adopted, and because of their historical weight, will still influence how people understand terms like *Infinite* or *Being*.

Instead of belaboring our words, let us focus instead on relinquishing old and outdated beliefs about reality and what it means to be human. In truth, the nomenclature only matters to the extent that it leads us to misperceptions or creates resistance in us. It is better that we simply accept the limits of our vocabulary and recognize that words are inadequate.

Throughout the book, I use the word *Light* because that is what I experience. I also use *Divine* and, on occasion, *God* to refer to something that exceeds our physical being and cannot be measured, but to which we are connected as the source of all life. I accept that these words carry their historical baggage, and it is only by learning to release those misconceptions that we can move forward without being weighed down by them. If those words create too much resistance for you, you may substitute other words, such as *Love* and *Universe*, as you read.

ENERGY

ONE BENEFIT OF USING THE WORD *LIGHT* is that it helps us to move beyond the idea of God as a physical being who looks like us, and invokes the sense that what we are really talking about is energy. This is not a new concept. We already use the word *light* as the energy of spiritual development in words such as *enlightenment* and *illumination*, or when we tell someone to "lighten up." People regularly send each other "love and light" as an expression of support. The same is true of other traditions: In Chinese medicine, life energy is referred to as *qi*, and in the Hindu tradition, *prana*.

The language of energy helps us move away from traditional concepts of the Divine. A basic tenet of science is that everything is made of energy. People, plants, animals, and inanimate objects all contain energy; some are more dynamic, others are more inert. We know this because matter is made up of smaller particles of energy, which come together to create different elements. This means, of course, that our minds and bodies are just forms of energy; for example, the heart uses electrical currents, which we can monitor with an EKG machine, and the brain percolates with electrical currents across its synapses. Our minds are likewise made of *energy*—the energy of our thoughts and emotions. This is a topic that we will explore further in subsequent chapters.

It can be helpful to some readers to use a word like *Light* or *energy*, which partakes of a scientific language. Some people only believe in aspects of spirituality that science has confirmed. For instance, studies now frequently validate pieces of spiritual wisdom that have existed for millennia, such as the benefits of meditation on the human mind and body. By no means is this to suggest that scientific validation is necessary for spirituality to have any meaning. Nor is science unassailable; science is always correcting itself as well, as it modifies and upends its previous conclusions. But borrowing from the language of science can help some to move beyond old paradigms of thinking.

Take, for example, the Higgs boson, sometimes called the God particle. Scientists first theorized that there was a field that existed everywhere in the universe, and the Higgs boson was the particle that connected every particle to that field and gave it mass; without the Higgs boson, we would literally not matter. For spiritually minded readers, the idea that a field exists everywhere in the universe and we are connected to it is hardly novel. That would be one way of conceptualizing the Light. For the more scientifically oriented, then, perhaps instead of thinking of the Light as some sort of mystical or magical force, you might think of it as the Higgs field: an energy field that runs throughout the entire fabric of the universe. From this perspective, science and spirituality can converge, albeit following different paths, in understanding the Light as the energetic matrix from which we are all created.

Birthright

I DO NOT JUST EXPERIENCE THE LIGHT; I also see it. The first time I saw the Light, I was staring at the floor when, out of the blue, very fast streams of light, almost like rain drops, started rushing past me in midair; I could see them clearly against the dark fabric of the carpet. At first I thought that it was raining, but there wasn't a cloud in the sky, and I wasn't even looking out the window! There were times I doubted what I had I seen, and times when I couldn't see the Light at all. Eventually, I came to realize that the Light was always there. It was simply easier to see when I was in a calm, peaceful state. At these times, I would become filled with an enormous sense of joy and happiness. It was like having a window open into another aspect of our world—a source of pure love and happiness that literally surrounded all of us.

Seeing the Light marked the beginning of my shift from a normal human being with lots of anger and anxiety to someone filled with joy, wonder, and mystical experiences that have nurtured a tremendous faith in life. Seeing the Light provided a visual confirmation that the world is not as we typically see it. However, I am hardly unique. Being connected to the Light is something that is available to each and every one of us.

People experience the Light all the time. Maybe not in that intense, direct sort of way, but they do experience that kind of bliss in their everyday lives. They just do not usually associate it with divinity or spirituality. People often feel moments of unconditional love in a relationship, especially with a child or a pet when there are no expectations and no conditions. For others, the sublime experience of nature or the aesthetic ecstasy of art or music affords a moment of utter peace or overwhelming joy. That same type of bliss can also come to people through seemingly miraculous creative inspiration—such as when you suddenly have a new and novel idea or breakthrough, and are so excited you can barely sit still. These are the moments in which thought turns to Light.

Most of the time, however, our minds are so busy that we cannot be present to the experience for more than a brief moment. Our connection with that energy is experienced as a jolt of pure bliss or a wave of absolute peace that quickly gives way to mental activity. You may have watched your child and been overwhelmed with pure love, only to suddenly think about the child's safety, and then became caught up in how to protect him or her. Or you may have stared at a waterfall and become mesmerized for some time, until suddenly you thought, *We'd better get moving or we'll miss lunch*, and the moment passed. Without the ability to recognize the bursts of love that you do experience, it is impossible to develop a sustained connection to the Light that does not depend on particular people or places for that connection.

Most of us are not taught that we can have a direct connection with the Light. This is one of the most damaging beliefs of our time. We were born to be enlighted. Our true state of being is one of unconditional love. Nothing else—anxiety, sadness, anger, or fear—is real. It is all an illusion made up by our minds. We have a tendency to spend our lives riddled with anxiety, too fearful of the future or resentful of the past to connect with that place of perfect peace that is within us. Most of our habits and thought patterns are self-defeating and negative. We repeat them over and over through the years, and they become engrained and resistant to change. They are entrenched thoughts that come from deeply rooted belief systems, and those thoughts cause us to react in ways that we often regret, or to take actions that lead us in a direction we don't want to go. As my experience confirms, we are all able to clear our minds of those toxic thoughts and open to the Light, that place of profound unconditional love that resides within all of us. How to connect to the Light is what this book endeavors to show you.

Begin to reflect on moments in your life when you felt utterly peaceful, ecstatically happy, or full of life. What did that peace, bliss, or fullness mean to you? Recall the circumstances under which those experiences took place. Is there something particular or special about those moments? Did you associate them at the time with God or the Divine?

Choose one of those moments to reflect on the experience. Do you recall any thoughts that were associated with that experience? How long did that peace or bliss last? Can you recall when and how that moment ended?

Think about someone you know or have met who seemed to exude love and happiness. How did you feel, being around that person? Did you wonder how or why they were able to emit that type of energy?

CHAPTER 2

EGO: SEPARATION FROM OUR TRUE SELF

*The "normal" state of mind
of most human beings contains
a strong element of what we might call
dysfunction or madness.*
— Eckhart Tolle, *A New Earth*

PART OF WHAT MAKES US uniquely human is the ego. When I first started experiencing the Light with Mirabai and Amma, the beautiful glow from a transmission or darshan would last a short while and then begin to fade. Old anxieties and worries would resurface, and self-defeating thoughts like, *Why can't I feel the Light any more?* would percolate in my head. *Was something wrong with me? Did I do something to make the Light go away?* I soon realized that the problem was not with me or anything I had done, but with the very voice that was asking those questions.

That voice was my ego, and that's where all of our problems start—in our minds. The ego is the part of you that says, "I am me. You are you. I am not you, and therefore you are not me." It is the part of you that draws boundaries between you and the rest of the physical world. This is known as *separation*. The ego, based on what our eyes can see, thinks that we are separate, autonomous individuals.

We need an ego to operate and survive in this world. Our minds allow us to think, speak, perceive objects, etc., and thereby to navigate time and space. Can you imagine how bad traffic would be if we couldn't distinguish where our car ended and another began? It's true that sometimes the ego gets an overly bad rap, but only sometimes. Most of the time, the ego becomes more than a healthy mechanism that allows us to interact with the physical world. It starts growing, hungry for fame and fortune and other substitutes for love, until it decides it's going to run the show. That's when the problems begin.

Because of our egos, we spend countless hours wondering and worrying about what might happen to us in the future or regretting what we did in the past. In addition, we talk incessantly about the past and the future to our family and friends, or anyone who will listen. We believe our thoughts to be true and react to the emotions that they generate. This creates a fantasy world that we believe to be real. We are all prisoners of our own minds. It is exhausting, which is why people spend so much time watching TV, surfing the Internet, drinking alcohol, and looking ahead to weekends where they can plan vacations. We are trying to escape our minds.

JUDGMENT

THE EGO IS FILLED WITH JUDGMENT. Our minds are constantly generating meaning, and more often than not, that meaning takes the form of judgment or evaluation.

As an experiment, watch your mind for a day and just observe how many of your thoughts are about liking or disliking something, viewing something as good or bad. How often did you find yourself putting whatever you saw, read, or heard into categories of right or wrong, good or bad? We like that which we think is right, and we dislike that which we think is wrong. How much of that good or bad thinking was directed at other people? Our egos generate a lot of judgment about others, characterizing them as bad, stupid, ugly, etc.

We can thank our egos for all of that mental and emotional anguish. The ego generates thoughts that we believe to be true, and we react emotionally to those thoughts. For example, let's say that you are leaving for vacation, but the traffic is terrible, and you realize that you are going to miss your flight. You *think* something like, *This is terrible. My vacation is going to be ruined. Who are all these stupid drivers on the road? Why does this always happen to me?* You follow up with an emotional response, probably disappointment, anger, or frustration.

The first thought is a judgment. This is a "bad" event, and the emotion arises in response to how bad you think it is to miss your flight. That first thought and emotional response leads to another thought: Because you will miss your flight, more bad luck will follow and your entire vacation will be ruined, not just briefly postponed. Your ego has now generated a thought for which there is no evidence; nothing else has suggested that your vacation is over, and you could probably get on the next flight. But now you feel even worse, so you then blame everyone else (it has to be someone's fault). Finally, the *coup de grâce*: It's about *me*. The ego asserts itself, suggesting that you are a perpetual victim of bad luck. You now feel awful and anxious, and perhaps begin to berate yourself mentally with statements like, *Why didn't I leave sooner? I always screw up. I'm so stupid!* What was nothing more than a possible delay in your flight has now become a diatribe about your worthiness as a person.

Imagine that you found out that you could get on the next flight an hour later, or that the flight you were originally on was going to crash, or that you would meet your future spouse on the later flight or in the airport during the delay. You would have an entirely different evaluation of how good or bad the flight delay was. You might even say that the missed flight turned out to be a "blessing in disguise." In response to that new information, your mind would begin to generate another set of thoughts and emotional reactions based on that new data, such as, *How lucky I am!* or *I am so blessed!* The ego can't help itself.

However, the ego doesn't direct its judgments toward only external events. Our egos save their worst vitriol for ourselves. The ego spits out a stream of constant thoughts that, unfortunately, often lead us to take unskillful and reactive actions in an attempt to escape the pain of whatever emotion we're experiencing. For example, let's say that someone tells you that you're overweight. Maybe you get angry and defensive and think or say something about *their* weight. Or maybe you think to yourself, *Yes, I am overweight*, and berate yourself. You then attempt to assuage that unhealthy emotion by consuming a pint of ice cream, which gives you only a temporary sense of comfort. After the momentary pleasure of eating fades, your ego enters the picture again, telling you that you have no will power, make terrible food choices, and have gained more weight.

Control

As the flight delay example reminds us, we are often not in control of our own minds. Further, most of us can't even acknowledge that we are not in control. We're constantly thinking about the past, projecting onto the future, and completely missing the present based on things that happened to us that we misunderstood in the first place. The simple fact is that when our egos are in charge, we don't really see what's happening right in front of us, right now.

Let's try another experiment. Sit quietly for five minutes and try not to think any thoughts at all. How long did you go without thinking? Did you make it more than a few seconds? Now try a different version of the same experiment. Pick one object or person to focus all of your thoughts on, and think about nothing else for five minutes. How much time passed before your mind drifted to something else?

For most people, the act of thinking about one thing or the act of not thinking will last at most a few seconds. How many of us have experienced hearing a song that we just can't get out of our head? Most of us can't turn it off because we are not in control of our minds.

This is the first step in recognizing that you are not your ego. The ego does its mind-controlling work by spinning a constant stream of thoughts and emotions. An incessant chatterbox, the ego never stops talking. Why are the thoughts so constant? Deep down, the ego knows that it is little more than a stream of thoughts that disappear with each passing second. The ego tries desperately to feel permanent and fixed through that constant chatter. *If I generate thoughts, I exist*, is the ego's mantra. Have you ever noticed how uncomfortable some people are if they aren't talking?

Boundaries

THE EGO HAS TO WORK CONSTANTLY at keeping you separate from others. Its primary mechanism is repulsion: The ego defines itself by what it is *not*. Try the same thought experiment as before and see how many times throughout a day (or even just an hour), your mind says, "I don't like ____." It can be anything, a person, place, or thing. It can even be what you experience in the media, be it in a newspaper, online websites, social media, or on television. Watch as your mind engages in the constant practice of discrimination: "I like this, I don't like that." Notice how much of your mind is preoccupied with saying, "I'm not those things that I don't like. That's not me."

The ego is establishing boundaries, separating you from the rest of the world by drawing a line between what the ego says you are and what it says you are not. For many of us, our thoughts of what we are not can be deeply and pervasively negative: *I am not good enough, I'm not lovable, I don't have approval from others, I don't have enough money, I'll never be healthy again, etc.* These negative thoughts are often repeated over and over.

Some of our repetitive thoughts may *seem* to be positive, and the ego also uses positive thoughts—

but not always for our highest good. This is known as *attachment*, which is the flipside of repulsion. You hold onto something to make you feel secure. In fact, many of our so-called positive thoughts are designed to keep deeply negative thoughts at bay. For example, what if you say to yourself, *I'm successful. I make a lot of money. I have a big house. I have a closet full of clothes.* Because you think that these objects provide a sense of economic security, then the underlying thought is actually fear. We are telling ourselves we're okay. Many of us seek abundance because we want to fill some sense of lack; we think that having a house, money, or a spouse means we are safe and secure.

IDENTITY

ONE OF THE WAYS FOR THE EGO to overcome that insecurity is to generate an identity. The ego is a storyteller that loves to generate stories about who we are, and those stories have many chapters, which ultimately form what we call an *identity*. We spin a first-person narrative: I was born here, this happened to me, I did this, I'm this sort of person, etc. In my case, for years I had fashioned an identity around being intelligent, and I had a strong attachment to that identity. My ego also thought that if I didn't live up to that identity, people would be disappointed in me. The Light had other plans for me, though.

Our ego doesn't just have one identity, however. We have multiple identities—different roles that we identify with and act out, depending on the circumstances. Many of those identities are roles that we all recognize. We have our work identity (I'm a lawyer, a business executive, a teacher, a police officer, etc.), our social identities (I'm a fun partier, I'm an art lover, I'm a political activist, I'm a creative type), and our relationship identities (I'm a husband, a wife, a boyfriend, a girlfriend, mother, father, sister, brother, etc.).

For example, being a mother is an incredibly strong identity for many women, and your mother's ego might have been strongly bound up in her image of what it meant to be a mother. She may have thought being a good mother meant that she had to do certain tasks or sacrifice some of her own dreams and pursuits. It may have meant that she thought the house had to look a certain way, that she could only wear her hair or clothes in a certain fashion in order to live up to this image, or that she had to perform certain tasks for you or your father as part of being a good mother. Anything that wouldn't fit the image of the good mother would be rejected as a threat to her ego's identity as a mother.

We all do this to ourselves. We all generate identities, and these are the masks that we present to the world. Not every aspect of who we are comes from the negative ego, but for many of us, the qualities that are the most authentic and truest parts of ourselves are *not* part of an identity or mask that we wear. We tend to hide those parts, because they are so precious to us, and we're afraid that others will judge us. For most of us, our identities are limited versions of what we could be. Those identities are rooted in defense mechanisms, early childhood trauma, family patterns of behavior, and cultural norms. In my case, my desire to be smart was the way I connected with my father and sought his approval. Behind that mask lies our true, authentic self. But the ego controls us, most often through negative emotions, to hide the divine self that we were born to become from our conscious selves.

FEAR AND RESISTANCE

WHY DOES THE EGO DO THIS? Deep down, the ego fears the loss of itself. For this reason, fear is the dominant emotion of the ego. Remember how the ego speaks in the language of separation, which says that we are separate, autonomous individuals? That belief in separation leads the ego to perceive everything as *me* or *mine* and the rest as *you* or *yours*. From the ego's point of view, what's mine could be taken from me and be made yours, and therefore what's mine is never truly and completely mine. *I* can always lose. This is the source of the idea that there is such a thing as lack or loss. Thus, the ego goes on to tell us that some of us are safe, and some of us are not; some of us are loved and worthy and successful and beautiful, and some of us are not. That is why the ego is often concerned about the future; loss is always only a moment away.

These negative emotions are actually rooted in the primal fear that you are unloved and unworthy of love. This is the aspect of the negative ego that keeps us from loving ourselves and others fully and unconditionally. While the ego can be overcome, whenever it is challenged, the first thing it does is resist. It feels threatened and will do what it can to protect itself. The ego puts up a strong fight, and you will find that it is crafty and capable of reemerging in unforeseen ways and places. The simplest measure of your ego being at play is any time you push back against or resist anything. The ego is very defensive, so any time that you rush to defend yourself from an accusation or a comment, your ego is doing the reacting.

Let's take an example that, in my experience, triggers people's egos in multiple ways: You are on the subway, heading home from work after a long day, and a homeless person begins to ask everyone on the train for spare change or some food to eat. Is your reaction, *Oh, thank goodness that's not me,* or *I hope s/he doesn't stop in front of me?* Those are ego-based responses. The first thought is repulsion, which is one of the two main responses of the ego. The thought the ego generates to secure its identity is, *That is not me.* The second is born out of fear and scarcity, of not wanting to give, despite the fact that you probably have enough money or food to share.

What would be a response that doesn't resist? A reaction like, *This person needs my help, and I will be of service in whatever way I can at this very moment,* is a heart-centered reaction born from compassion. You recognize that homelessness is an injustice that should be rectified and that no one should go hungry. It does not resist the situation and does not attempt to create distance between you and the homeless person. This sort of response acknowledges the situation instead of your ego.

But the ego is wily. It will attempt to reassert itself at every moment. If, after you've stopped to help, your thought process is, *Why isn't any one else offering to help? Everyone else is so self-centered*, or, if the homeless person refuses your help or doesn't seem particularly grateful, and you think, *Well, why bother? If s/he can't appreciate some help, no wonder s/he's homeless!*, your ego is again at play. It has found a way to reiterate its sense of a boundary between you and others. Your ego wanted to establish that you're better than others because you're helping and others are not, or that it has an expectation of thanks that was not met by the recipient of your generosity.

The negative ego is a relentless master and a devious liar. It tells us that we are not safe or secure, that we are not loved, and asks us to hide our true selves and wear instead an image crafted to please others. A means by which to survive in the physical world, the ego has become instead the very thing that keeps us from connecting with the Light. In the name of survival and approval, our egos play a cruel game, depriving us of our capacity to experience unconditional love. That is a game that we cannot win. It is only when you give up that game, and accept who you truly are, that you can begin to dismantle the negative ego.

Take a moment to pause and reflect on your own mind. Do you recognize some of these mechanisms in your own thoughts? See where you draw lines to separate yourself from others. Notice how often you say "I like" or "I dislike." Begin to see the ways in which your ego divides up the world into you and everyone else, good and bad, right and wrong.

Do you tend to focus on the past or the future? Do you regard the past with regret or nostalgia? Do you regard the future with anxiety or excitement?

Can you think of examples where you thought something was terrible, and later quite fortunate? What changed?

What types of identities do you hold onto? What aspects of yourself, if challenged by another person, would cause you to feel defensive or attacked? What aspects of yourself, if you had to give them up or they turned out not to be true, would cause you the most pain?

CHAPTER 3

BELIEFS: WE BECOME WHAT WE THINK

*Belief is a phantom that the mind has made real
that has nothing to do with You,
the real You, the true You.*
— William Linville, *Living in a Body on a Planet*

IMAGINE THAT YOU GO INTO a coffee shop or restaurant and find a tip jar on the counter that reads, "Tipping is good karma." The message is that if you give you will reap benefits, and if you don't give you won't. What is your reaction to that statement? Do you give begrudgingly, unhappy that your latte is even more expensive, or mindlessly, out of habit? Do you give enthusiastically, thinking that you're helping out a person who may not be making a lot of money?

However we choose to react, our response to the tip jar scenario is a reflection of our beliefs. If we give begrudgingly, we may be saying to ourselves, *I don't believe in karma*, or perhaps, *I don't have extra money for tips*, or even, *Baristas are greedy*. Each of those responses reflects a belief about karma, your financial welfare, or the reasons why baristas might want tips. If we give because we are expected to give and do not want to seem selfish, that is a response based on a belief in the need to appear to be a good person.

Almost everything we say and do is the product of our mind's beliefs about the world. Our egos are programmed with a series of beliefs that produce our thoughts. Those beliefs are often rooted in what we have been taught by family and society. In addition, each thought you have carries with it the energy of your emotional response to that thought. In the example above, the emotional energy may have been disdain or judgment if you disliked the tipping jar, or gratitude if you felt that tipping was a good thing to do. Collectively, your thoughts and emotions produce an energetic state—what we might call your "vibrational frequency."

Frequency and Manifestation

We can "feel" energy vibrate at a particular frequency. Have you ever entered a room and thought, *The tension is so thick I could cut it with a knife*? That's because the energy of tension is thick and dense. All of us know that fear feels a certain way and that love feels quite different. For example, suppose we think that someone dear to us has been hurt. We feel anguish or sorrow, and we also experience these emotions in the body as a tightness or constriction in the throat, chest, or stomach. For another example, suppose someone insults us, and we think to ourselves that we are flawed or worthless. We may feel sad or depressed, and our body might feel heavy or even hot—the sort of flush associated with shame or embarrassment. That feeling reflects the fact that the emotion has a certain (low) frequency of energy. By contrast, when we feel loved, supported, or comforted, and have a sense of purpose, we feel lighter, happier, and more energized. The frequency of those emotions is higher.

We not only experience this energy in our own body, but are also aware of the energy of others. In fact, it is easier to understand vibrational frequency when you think about others. It can be difficult to be around someone who is anxious, depressed, or angry. It can be draining, because their emotional state is affecting your own frequency. Similarly, we know how uplifting it can be to be around certain people who seem to exude happiness and joy. Again, their frequency affects us, and in turn, we feel lighter and happier. You likely have friends or know people that always lift your spirits, and conversely, people who always seem to bring you down. That's vibrational frequency.

Why do we care about frequency? The vibrational frequency of your thoughts is directly correlated with the reality that you experience. Everything we think, say, or do emanates a particular frequency. The combined emotional energy of our ego's constant stream of thoughts creates our vibrational state. That vibrational state creates our experience of life; it draws to us people, opportunities, and events. Do you notice how some people are bursting with life and always seem to be enjoying new adventures and exciting successes, while others can't seem to catch a break, and are always dealing with one drama after another? The difference is their frequency.

This principle is now commonly known as the Law of Attraction. The popularization of the concept of frequency through the Law of Attraction has given people a powerful tool to manifest wealth by focusing positive intentions on a new job, more money, or a better relationship. There is, of course, nothing wrong with manifesting abundance. The problem is when it perpetuates a paradigm of materialism over spirituality, or worse still, creates a sense that the Divine is nothing more than a cosmic Amazon.com, ready to ship us what we want as soon as we ask for it with enough positivity.

Another, more traditional term for this principle of vibrational frequency is *karma*. This is the common explanation for why we must endure all the strife and struggle that seem to comprise human existence: The energy we put into the world eventually returns to us, and if that energy was negative, we typically end up being confronted with negative repercussions of our prior actions. That is, we eventually reap the karmic seeds that we have sown, including actions from past lives. That energy doesn't disappear. It returns again, in a different form, but of the same frequency as that which you emitted.

Whether we think in terms of the Law of Attraction or karma, the fundamental principle is that low-frequency emotions attract other low-frequency energy, and high-frequency emotions attract similar high-frequency energy. For example, perhaps you worry about what other people think of you and constantly seek their approval. This is a fairly common emotional pattern. You think to yourself, *They don't approve of me, so I am going to prove them wrong.* At your job then, you might find yourself agreeing to take on certain work assignments, perhaps more than you should, because you worry that you'll offend someone if you turn them down. Or perhaps you want to be heroic and perform some incredible feat that will garner you lots of accolades from your boss and peers. You then take on too many assignments and find yourself struggling to do the work at the caliber that it requires, exhausting yourself in the process. Perhaps you turn in work that is not quite as good as it could be, or you're late with it. The result is that you end up not getting the sort of approval you wanted in the first place. Alternatively, you exhaust yourself completing all of these assignments and *do* get the approval you seek, but are miserable in the process. This approval mechanism often leads to the opposite of what you were seeking, although it gave you confirmation of what you believed in the first place: that you did not have the approval of others.

Another quite common scenario is when people are addicted to drama. Have you ever wondered why some people are always dealing with drama? Some part of them is creating it because their thoughts and words are all expressing drama. They are perpetually concerned and talking about what's going to happen to them, what so-and-so said to them, why such-and-such person was mean to them. They draw to them the very drama that they complain about. These people never seem to catch a break; every time they appear to turn a corner and life starts to improve, something else comes crashing down. As much as you want to care for and help these people, it is important to recognize that they draw this strife into their lives, either consciously or unconsciously. Fixing whatever problem comes up won't get to the core of the problem, and more often than not, will simply exhaust you when you are enmeshed in low-frequency energy.

FAMILIAL AND CULTURAL BELIEFS

IF WE WANT TO TRANSFORM OUR THOUGHTS and emotional responses, we must root out the belief systems that give rise to them in the first place. The majority of those belief systems are limiting, self-sabotaging, and rooted in past trauma.

Many of our beliefs come from our parents, grandparents, siblings, and even extended family over the course of our lifetime. Some of those beliefs have been passed down and reinforced for generations. This is why so many of us come to resemble our parents as we age; we replicate the patterns that we have been taught, and those inherited views often shape how we experience life.

Many families deal with longstanding and pervasive beliefs around topics like money, politics, or emotional expression. For example, suppose your parents worked low-paying jobs and struggled to put food on the table. They might have made statements like, "Money doesn't come easy," or "Life is a struggle." You, in turn, may have inherited the same beliefs and find yourself struggling with money. You might even find yourself repeating those same statements, reflecting your (unconscious) adoption of those beliefs, or taking actions consistent with them. In all likelihood, you find that your life is a struggle and then say to yourself, "Well, Dad always said that life is a struggle." Ideally, some parents instill in their children a deep belief in their own abilities or life in general. For example, your parents may have told you that you would succeed if you "followed your heart," or that you should "never give up on your dreams." As a result, you may have a much stronger sense of purpose in life, with the ability to weather challenges with greater ease than some of your friends and coworkers. You can no doubt easily identify any number of beliefs about how the world works that you have inherited from your parents.

Nor are our beliefs limited to our family or lineage. Changing our patterns of thought requires us to understand how our belief systems have been formed by our social norms and cultural practices. We come into this world categorized by race, gender, nationality, and class. All of these are conditions that we inherit and have to contend with. In my case, each of those categories is attached to a series of cultural beliefs about what it means to be a gay, white American male from a lower-middle class background. Our society teaches us certain beliefs about what is normal or traditional, and these beliefs often form our understanding of what we "should" or "should not" do. Everything from food, to how to handle relationships, to the ways to make a living is a reflection of cultural norms. Many of our patterns and habits are based on our perception of how we fit into society; we dress, speak, act, and reside in certain places, according to our perceptions of who we are and where we belong. As a society, we have built structures

and organizations—legal, political, and economic—
based on those collective beliefs.

Consider gender roles, for example. For
millennia, men and women have had to navigate
appropriate norms of behavior about the type of
clothing they should wear and how they should behave,
and more importantly, beliefs about the relative value
of men and women. In the past, women were not able
to own property or vote. They have faced enormous
discrimination, and even today there remain deeply
entrenched views about gender that account for pay
discrepancies and limited job opportunities. None of
those norms has any real truth other than that we have
agreed to them.

Sex is another example. Our culture adheres
to many pernicious beliefs about sex—when we should
have it, with whom, and what your sexual practices
say about you. We have lots of words for people who
really enjoy sex. Our society imposes a great deal of
stigma, even criminal liability, on those who accept
money for it. Gay men used to face the criminal justice
system for having consensual sex. All of these views are
collective beliefs about what is proper. When same-sex
marriage began to become legalized, people opposed to

homosexuality stated that marriage was the bedrock of civilization and that society would collapse if two men or women could marry. Now that gay couples have been marrying, new norms are evolving, and people who previously opposed same-sex marriage now accept and recognize that their opposition was based on fear.

Unfortunately, so many of those belief systems and structures reflect the collective fears of our egos. A cursory glance at any newspaper reveals headlines about political partisanship, immigration, racial and sexual discrimination, gun-related violence, income inequality, and climate change. Each of those topics inevitably reflects some normative view of how one ought to live or some fear about a lack of resources. If you believe all of it, you might come to the view that the world is a cruel and terrible place. Now try to live a prosperous and happy life coming from that belief.

Unconscious Beliefs

ALL TOO OFTEN, OUR WORDS and actions end up reinforcing certain beliefs. For example, if you believe that friends will always let you down, you may even engage in behavior that tests and sabotages them, thus confirming your belief that friends always let you down. As a result, our beliefs and actions create a sort of feedback loop, and we further entrench ourselves in patterns of thought and action that are self-defeating. The result is that our belief systems are *sticky*; they are hard to uproot.

Even more pernicious, many of our beliefs are unconscious. We don't even know that we're thinking and reacting to certain views of the world. This is one of the reasons why positive thinking alone is not enough. In fact, many of us want to believe that our thoughts are primarily rooted in love rather than fear, and that we are therefore vibrating at a higher frequency. We focus intently on positive thoughts (everything's great, I'm healthy, I'm happy, etc.) as indications of our vibrational state. Unfortunately, this is often not the case. For some that may be true, but because many people have not uprooted their unconscious beliefs, they are actually vibrating at a lower frequency.

Because our beliefs are unconscious, many people are constantly sending out contradictory and often unconscious thoughts about what they want. For example, they may want a new job or career, but they're constantly changing their minds about exactly what they think that should look like, which makes it difficult for the job to manifest. When we are anxious and worry about money, we might consciously be saying, "I want more money," or "I am abundant," but energetically, the thoughts are vibrating at a lower frequency, so it is as if we are saying, "I don't have enough."

These underlying thoughts (rooted in fear) are what Neale Donald Walsch refers to as "sponsoring thoughts," and are the real energy behind our thinking.[1] That's the energy that is going to call forth what you experience as your reality. To put it differently, you might be saying, "I need more money," and yet your belief system is that money is the root of all evil. In that situation, how abundant can you possibly be?

Fear is the underlying frequency for many people's thoughts and beliefs. As a result, many of us continuously create problems in our lives through our unconscious thoughts, poorly chosen or emotionally charged words, and from precipitous and reactive actions all rooted in a deep underlying fear. Driven by fear, we often make choices that are primarily concerned with our own security and success—at the expense of the security and success of everyone else. Ironically, most of what we fear is fear itself. We can't bring ourselves to really examine our fear or experience that emotion. Many of us want to make certain changes in our lives, do something different with our careers, or connect with others. But the fear of failure or the fear of rejection often creates paralysis. We don't take the actions we need to fulfill those desires. The paralysis comes from our *avoidance* of that fear, and so we create a life designed to keep that fear at bay.

Why do we feel so much fear? For many of us, the underlying root of most fear-based thoughts and actions is a deep belief in our own unworthiness. Deep down, we think we are not worthy of anything (love, life, happiness, etc.), and we don't approve of ourselves; so we seek an external source of approval to squelch that inner lack. This leads us to seek the approval of others. As Buddhist spiritual teacher and writer, Ezra Bayda, lucidly puts it, "The belief is, 'If I can get you to like me, I won't have to feel the pain of being unworthy.'"[2] What unworthiness generates is the fear that love will be withdrawn if our unworthiness is exposed. Approval tells us that we're okay, that we're liked, that the person who likes us will not withdraw their love and affection. But approval is short-lived; the feeling of inadequacy returns the next time we do something that may cause someone to disapprove of us. This cycle of fear and unworthiness generates a great deal of self-loathing.

No one is worthless or unlovable. That is, of course, the lie the ego tells us. Nevertheless, most of us monitor our behavior and choose actions based on what we *think* others expect or want from us. Our words and actions no longer stem from an authentic place within us, but rather are designed to maintain an image or projection. Beneath that shell sits our core sense of unworthiness, kept at bay. Often it becomes a deeper longing and remorse derived from not living authentically. If there is a single frequency at which most people are vibrating unconsciously, it is at the frequency of unworthiness. Most of us live our lives aligned with the expectations of others, and in the process, rarely if ever experience life in complete alignment with our souls.

Feelings of unworthiness are also the main block in accessing the Light. Many people believe that they are not worthy of God's love. Just as our ego tells us we are separate from each other, so too does it tell us that we are separate from God and in no way connected to the Divine. Instead, we perceive that God is in some nether realm, watching and judging from afar. We think bad things happen to us because we are deeply flawed, and God appropriately punishes us for those flaws. As a result, we believe that God, through judgment of our supposed misdeeds, is responsible for anything negative that happens in our life. We believe that if only we can conform to certain behaviors and norms, we won't incur God's wrath, and will be loved and forgiven; otherwise, we are condemned. Therefore, we engage in the most epic confusion—we equate everything negative that happens to us with God's punishment.

UNCONDITIONAL LOVE

WHEN WE DON'T FEEL LOVED, we have a hard time responding with love. This is quite common in our relationships. Perhaps you have a close friend or a sibling who upsets you in some way. Your wounded ego is not capable of recognizing that this person was speaking or acting from a place of fear or shame created by *their* ego. As a result, you respond with negativity rather than with compassion. And the constant exchange of negativity continues, until the relationship deteriorates or perhaps even ends.

The challenge that life presents is to overcome this myth of separation; our purpose is to raise the frequency of our consciousness to be able to respond to all people and events in our life from a place of unconditional love. This means not only in loving a partner, a family member, or a pet, but responding with love to everyone and everything that happens to you. To put it another way, our purpose is to become the Light. Imagine how your world would be if every thought, word, and deed were motivated by love rather than fear or anger. What if you were grateful for everything that occurred instead of resisting or resenting it? Your entire world would be transformed. Now imagine what that would look like on a global scale. It would be heaven on earth.

Another word for this state of unconditional love is *enlightenment*. Like *God*, it's a word with a lot of baggage. Contrary to some preconceived ideas, enlightenment does not mean we sit around all day meditating. We must still fulfill our responsibilities and take care of our physical needs. Doing so from a place of love is part of fulfilling life's purpose. To love everyone and everything simply means that we do not judge them. We do not deem them bad or inferior or less worthy of love. Rather, we see everyone as an utterly perfect creation that is worthy of complete abundance, happiness, and health. It is the state of wanting everyone we encounter to enjoy his or her highest good, even when someone is expressing anger, fear, or behaving violently.

Here is an uplifting example of this practice. I once encountered someone in the workplace who had a reputation for being a mean and angry person. This individual was feared by coworkers—subordinates and equals alike. Although I was warned that working with this person was often a stressful experience, I chose not to prejudge this person based solely on their reputation. Rather than meeting them in the past, I insisted upon meeting this person in the present. There were certainly moments of interaction that could have led me to conclude that my colleagues were right, but I continued to respond to this person from a place of love. Over time, our relationship developed into one of mutual respect and affection. I learned that there was a tremendous amount of love in this person that was just waiting to be shared.

Unconditional love does not mean that we permit people to do harm to us or anyone else. As the poet Mark Nepo writes, "Unconditional love does not require a passive acceptance of whatever happens in the name of love. Rather, in the real spaces of our daily relationships, it means we maintain a commitment that no condition will keep us from bringing all of who were are to each other honestly."[3] We often confuse a response based on love with a response that seeks approval; you can say no to someone and still regard the person with love. You simply don't judge them or think of them as unworthy, despite whatever action they have taken that requires you to draw a boundary.

Another example from my professional life: I briefly worked for someone whose judgment and skills I did not trust. This person took a cavalier approach to sensitive issues and did not seem to care about the consequences for others. My intuition urged me to leave the job as quickly as possible. I did not stay out of some sense of approval or belief that love required me to continue to occupy the same space as this person. But in leaving, I took care not to condemn this person, make them wrong, or make them the cause of my departure; I simply left and wished that person good luck with their business.

It is not easy to rid ourselves of belief systems that we have used our entire lives, but that is what we must all learn to do. It is not easy to accept the vulnerability that comes with responding with love to all that we encounter. I have certainly had my share of what some might see as "failures"—former friends, ex-partners, and roommates, where our egos clashed and neither of us was spiritually awake enough to avoid deeply hurting the other. Those lessons will still need to be repeated until we learn. We often fall back into certain patterns, particularly where a relationship already exists with certain expectations of how each person will behave. That is why negative karma returns to us; it affords us the opportunity to respond to that negative energy with the love that should have been our response in the first place. When you have little practice at responding with love but a lot of practice at responding with fear, it is easy to fall prey to fear. For most of us, it will be the practice of a lifetime.

There is a powerful statement that has long been attributed to Jesus Christ: "What you do unto others, you do unto yourself." There is no *I* without a *you*. The *I* is nothing more than a web of connections, of relationships. What we perceive in others is really a projection onto others of something in ourselves. This is the opening to unconditional love: to realize that regardless of the ways in which we are all governed by our egos, and despite all the apparent differences, we are all the same. Any belief that others are actually separate from us is an optical illusion created by our eyes. We are actually just vibrating energy coming into contact with other vibrations of energy. What you see is a reflection of your own frequency. Our task is to confront again and again that illusion of separation and meet it with the frequency of unconditional love.

Pause here to ponder what beliefs about life and about yourself are shaping the life that you lead. Can you identify at least one belief that you inherited from your parents? Are there cultural, political, or religious beliefs that govern your actions?

Make a list of any deeply held beliefs about yourself. It can be hard to admit that we don't always love ourselves completely or that we are often our own worst critic. Be gentle with yourself as you begin to see the belief systems that are running your life.

CHAPTER 4

ALIGNMENT: HOW WE
HEAL OURSELVES

*Each day your intention needs to be
to align your frequency
to the highest available to you.*
— Paul Selig, *The Book of Love and Creation*

IN THE FILM *THE LAST SAMURAI*, an American soldier, Captain Nathan Algren, is conscripted to do battle with the last remaining Japanese Samurai warriors. After the Samurai capture him, their leader, Katsumoto, stands before a cherry tree and tells him that a person could spend his or her entire life looking for the perfect cherry blossom and it would not be a wasted life.

At the end, in battle with American troops, Katsumoto suffers a fatal wound, and as Captain Algren (who has since joined the Samurai way of life) holds him in his arms, the wind blows through a cluster of cherry trees at the edge of the battlefield. Katsumoto watches the blossoms fall, and whispers with his last breath, "Perfect. They are all perfect."

The wisdom of Katsumoto's remarks is two-fold. It is true that a life spent trying to be the best version of yourself, to seek the perfect cherry blossom, is not a wasted life. It is equally true that the supposedly "imperfect" cherry blossoms are in fact already perfect; every life, no matter how flawed it may seem, is actually perfect just as it is. The beauty of Katsumoto's wisdom is that these are not separate principles. For most of us, living a life in which we embrace the truth that we are perfect just as we are, requires us to undertake spiritual practices to undo the parts of ourselves that tell us so persuasively just how imperfect we are. The key is to shift our perception so that we see ourselves as perfect just as we are and, at the same time, recognize that our ego can get in the way of that perception. Instead of thinking of ourselves as either flawed or divine, we can think of ourselves as fluctuating in and out of alignment with the frequency of the Light.

Healing

When we align with the Light, we are connected to an energy that vibrates at a much higher frequency than we have ever experienced. That high-frequency energy connects to and begins to speed up the much lower frequency of our bodies and minds. Low-frequency energies attract illness, misfortune, anger, and negativity from others. Physical and mental illness, unhappy relationships, and a life filled with crises and drama are all rooted in thoughts and actions of a low frequency. When we are connected to the Light, our minds and bodies release those lower, denser energies, and in particular the dense vibration of fear, and replace them with higher vibrations. We experience that higher frequency in our bodies as heat, tingling, electricity, and through the emotions of love, tenderness, peace, and bliss.

Alignment with the Light leads naturally and inexorably to healing. Because you are already perfect, any disease or disorder is born from the belief that you are somehow not perfect. The well-known spiritual guide, *A Course in Miracles*, tells us that all healing is, at its essence, the release from fear.[1] We generally think of healing as relief from a physical or emotional ailment and a return to the state of normalcy. From a spiritual perspective, healing means something more. The etymology of the word *healing* locates a possible origin in an Old English word *hal*, which means "to make whole." In fact, a modern-day definition of healing is to return to a state of "wholeness."[2] To be made whole is to remove the fear that you can be in a state of lack or loss.

Healing occurs by removing the fear that gave rise to the particular condition or illness. The primary causes of disease are thoughts of separation, unworthiness, and lack of love. Since our deepest underlying fear is that we are not loved or worthy of love, the way to remove fear is to become connected again with the Light, to strip away any belief that you are not whole and not already healed. Love—divine or unconditional love—is what eliminates that fear.

For most of us, it is not easy to accept that our minds create illness, largely because the reverse does not appear to ring true. When we get sick, we generally cannot *will* ourselves into good health or think ourselves out of disease. The reason is quite simple: Most of us lack the tools to undo the belief systems and patterns of thought that led to the illness in the first place. We have not trained our own minds to heal. This also explains why people have chronic conditions that come back repeatedly—because the underlying beliefs and subconscious emotions that gave rise to the illness were never resolved. As a result, traditional approaches to healing focus on alleviating symptoms, not eliminating root causes. While pharmaceutical medicine and surgery can be useful or even critical for healing acute situations, if the root fear has not been healed, the disease or ailment often returns in some form.

Healing is always a product of free will. You can choose *not* to heal, and that is what many people do. Those lower frequencies are there for a reason. We feel safe with the familiar, and most of us are constantly reproducing versions of what we already know; we replicate our past again and again. In many ways, we are attached to our illness, because we are still attached to the beliefs that formed them. Those beliefs may be the framework from which the ego has viewed the world throughout your entire life. As a result, when the Light begins to raise the vibration of the lower frequencies in your body and energy field, you may have internal resistance to that clearing.

Life for me did not instantly become full of bliss and grace. Instead, opening to the Light was the start of an immense period of turmoil, fear, and upheaval, as various parts of my life were being cleared.

For example, when I first began working with Mirabai, I was overwhelmed by the bliss, but the next day, my anxiety and fear would return. I didn't fully understand at the time how the Light worked or what I needed to do. I was expecting a miraculous, instantaneous healing. While miracles happen (what we call Divine grace), the belief that the Light should heal us instantaneously overlooks the fact that we can resist healing, or that our healing requires more time because we have important lessons to learn. Because healing didn't happen immediately for me, I thought that I couldn't be healed or that the Light refused to heal me. Eventually, I learned that the Light can be blissful and miraculous, but it cannot work without our assistance and willingness. That is the gift of free will. Through our choices we can block the Light from helping us; we can continue to sabotage ourselves.

Today I have never been healthier and happier, mentally and physically. In particular, the Light has been enormously healing for me on an emotional level, in regard to approval issues, fear of making mistakes and being punished, fear of what others think of me, and fear of being disliked or ignored. Worries about money and resources have radically diminished or disappeared altogether from my life. I also had a powerful clearing of a profound fear of the supernatural that I had acquired as a child from watching horror films and reading scary books. During the clearing, my mind was flooded with childhood memories and images, along with the fear associated with those images. It was a frightening experience, as if I were reliving all of those scary moments condensed into a brief period of time. Eventually, the fear subsided, and I could experience those memories without any emotional reaction, from a place of equanimity. On another occasion, I experienced a period of intense sadness, where I was extremely emotional, yet still filled with the most blissful Light. I realized that I was releasing a tremendous amount of sadness that I had held on to for other people, and the burden of their emotions was finally being released from my body.

Physical changes have been profound as well. Long-standing issues with blood sugar and asthma have greatly improved or been eliminated. I am no longer as afflicted with frequent sinus infections, which had led me to take lots of decongestants and antibiotics. My diet changed over time as well, as my body began to reject many toxic foods, such as factory-farmed meat and processed foods that contain no real nutrients.

The ways in which the Light heals are not always clear to us, nor do they unfold in the way we might expect. This is largely because we do not fully understand the real reasons why we experience physical and mental problems. The root causes are often buried deep within our mental and emotional patterns. For example, the pain we are experiencing in one part of our body may actually be related to emotional problems connected to certain members of our family.

In many instances, other issues that seem unrelated to your primary concern need to be cleared first. Emotional issues that we don't even realize are related may come up first. This may take a while to resolve, causing you to question why you are not healing. We may be unable to move forward with a romantic relationship due to the limiting belief that we are unlovable; this can be rooted in some childhood trauma, such as when a parent punished us for some wrongdoing. Because we cannot grasp the full picture of our lives (or lifetimes, if you accept the concept of reincarnation), what the Light brings us is not always what we think we need.

For example, at a time when I was trying to figure out the next step in my career, a case of plantar fasciitis emerged. Although the pain would be intermittent, none of the standard treatments did much to heal it. It was only when I came to understand that I wasn't feeling like I had a lot of support for my next steps (literally, because I was still working through some trust issues) that the physical manifestation through my foot made sense. As I worked through the trust issues and recognized the ways in which I was deeply supported in my life path by friends, family, and the Light, my body started to heal. My emotional state was then matching my physical state, and as one healed, so did the other.

Healing is an ongoing process of working through many layers of patterns of thought and belief systems that are ultimately rooted in fear and lack of lovability. As you deepen your connection to the Light, more and more unresolved issues from your past will arise for you to work on releasing. These can be rooted in either past lives or the present one.

Mystical Experiences

Our connection with the Light is not limited to healing in the more traditional sense of eliminating physical or emotional infirmities. Along with healing those issues, the Light also allows us to heal more fundamental issues, such as our belief in our separation from other people, or our belief that physical reality is what it appears to be to the naked eye. Instead, we realize how magnificent and amazing we truly are as human beings, and how little our potential is generally expressed. In other words, if we think of healing as being made whole by restoring our innate connection with the Light, then we realize that one of our most limiting beliefs is about the kinds of experiences we are able to have in a human body.

Changing that belief has led to extraordinary mystical experiences that have fundamentally altered how I view reality—and how I experience life. While I studied as an apprentice to Mirabai Devi, my body became increasingly able to receive higher amounts and frequencies of Light, and to remain connected to that Light longer.

On several occasions, I have experienced episodes of *samadhi*, a blissful union with the Light where there is no longer any thought or sense of self. My body is often percolating with energy, and I feel enormous charges of electricity coming through my hands whenever I bless my food or mentally bless another person. During Light transmissions with Mirabai or even periods of deep meditation, I experience *kriyas*, shakes or spasms that occur when the Light moves through denser energy in my body.

After one particularly powerful episode of *samadhi*, I met with the gifted intuitive, Tony LeRoy, who quickly intuited that my body was actually shedding the karmic build-up of my father's lineage. As he put it, the reasons my soul had chosen my father and his lineage for my incarnation in this lifetime were now complete. Therefore, I was releasing that karma. It made complete sense to me: My father had always had a difficult time with his heart and all of his identity was rooted in his intelligence, and I had emulated that karmic pattern during my lifetime. The Light healed this pattern by removing a tremendous amount of fear and damage that had been stored in my physical body and energy field throughout my life.

These examples of mystical experiences are being shared because as a highly rational person, I would not have believed them had I not experienced them myself. Instead, they have offered me a direct and personal window into the transformative energy of the Light. This grace is available to all of us. The Light heals us by making (a part of) us whole again. As my experience confirms, healing is also a product of free will. We can choose to heal and be made whole, or we can choose separation and lack. We can choose to align with the frequency of the Light, or stay in the lower frequency of the negative ego. That choice is what makes us uniquely human.

COLLECTIVE HEALING

TO ALIGN WITH THE FREQUENCY of the Light, with the frequency of unconditional love, is not a selfish undertaking; it is a critical step in our collective transformation. We live in a culture that is profoundly solipsistic, that emphasizes the acquisition of material goods and constant electronic communication and connectivity. Our world encourages ego gluttony and spiritual famine. We are spiritually starving ourselves in a way that is making this world unsustainable. Economic inequality and climate change are two of the largest indicators of how our collective egos have decided that only a few should have more than enough resources and that we can squander with impunity all that our planet provides us. We have fashioned a world where convenience and self-interest rein over compassion and empathy. Healing the enormous damage we have done to ourselves and to the earth requires each of us to transform ourselves internally.

To experience the transformative grace of the Light, we must fully embrace the truth that everybody is completely and totally worthy of love. No one is disconnected from the Light, from the universal consciousness that flows through all living beings. This is the fundamental truth that makes us all not only equal, but one and the same. In recent years, many spiritual writers and leaders have been teaching humanity's "oneness," or the idea that we are all interconnected. We are all connected in the physical world that shares the same planet; what we do in one area of the globe affects people everywhere. That is why climate change is a critical issue at this juncture in our lives. The damage to the planet is the pernicious effect of our actions with total disregard as to how they affect all life on this planet. It is now crucial that we work collectively to undo the damage.

Our planet is indeed undergoing a transition. This means that we must each make the decision to diminish our negative ego and embrace our connection with the Light. That means we must be aware of how our connection to others affects everyone else's vibrational frequency. What we think, say, and do—our collective frequency—reverberates throughout the energy fields of everyone else. We can literally assist in raising the frequency of everyone we come into contact with. Conversely, each of us can lower another person's frequency. This shift or ascension is a collective endeavor. We must make the most of every opportunity to open ourselves to the Light. As we raise our frequency, our thoughts and actions shift, and over time, the unjust behaviors and systems that were created through those thoughts and actions also shift. By doing so, we all contribute to humanity's collective transformation.

Pause here and reflect on any physical and emotional wounds you have had that were difficult to heal. Did they come back after initially appearing to go away?

Consider the possibility that all healing and disease stems from our underlying beliefs and emotional responses. Does this challenge your own belief system about how disease occurs or the power of emotions?

Does the idea of alignment with a certain type of energy or frequency appeal to you? How does it challenge some of your closely held beliefs about the nature of reality?

PART 2
TRANSFORMATION

CHAPTER 5

MEDITATION: LOOKING CLOSELY AT OUR MINDS

Meditation practice improves your life
by showing you, first of all,
with some difficult clarity, the mess you are in.
— Norman Fischer, *Taking Our Places*

THERE IS PERHAPS NO IMAGE of meditation more iconic than that of the Buddha sitting beneath the Bodhi tree, seeking to obtain enlightenment. Born a prince who led a sheltered life, Siddhartha Gautama left his palace walls to see true suffering in his people. Once he learned of how immense his people's suffering was, he set forth to find a way for all to escape suffering. After realizing that intense practices of asceticism (whereby he ate little and flogged his body) were not the way, Gautama sat beneath the Bodhi tree and meditated, vowing to attain enlightenment. After some forty-nine days of meditation, he overcame illusion, experienced the loss of self, and became the Buddha.

Fast-forward to the present day, and meditation has become all the rage. No longer an esoteric practice associated with the Buddha, meditation has been repackaged as a self-improvement technique. Newspapers and blogs applaud its many benefits, and it's often presented as a way to be more productive and less stressed. A cynical person might say that meditation is no longer about enlightenment, but about coping with capitalism.

The upshot is that meditation is now a mainstream practice. No one needs to abandon their work or families and enter a cave or an ashram and meditate all day to receive its benefits. But being more productive and less stressed are only a tiny portion of what meditation can provide. Meditation is a powerful tool for transformation because it allows you to realize that you are not your thoughts. The real you is not your ego. Your life will change as a result, but not because you leave it all behind or find a way to better cope with it. Your life transforms with meditation because you transform your relationship to your thoughts, and in doing so, your relationship to the world around you.

Muddy Waters

Ezra Bayda offers a useful analogy: Think of your mind as a glass of dirty water that has been stirred up.[1] With meditation, the water settles and slowly but surely the sediment or dirt begins to fall to the bottom, leaving still, clear water. Your thoughts are the dirt, and the "real" you is the clear water. This clear water is the Light, or what Buddhism calls the witnessing consciousness—the part of you that watches those thoughts. The clear water contains those thoughts, but so much mental agitation is being stirred up that you can't separate the dirt from the water. With meditation, the churning stops and the dirt settles to the bottom, leaving the water clear again. Meditation thus allows you to separate the water from the mud of your mind, and to begin to distance yourself from your ego's incessant thinking. This is the first step toward clearing your mind of negative thoughts.

Eliminating negative thought patterns is not an easy task. Many books simply tell the reader to ask for divine assistance or stay in the present moment. As legitimate as that advice may be, it has been reduced to an intellectual formula; our minds are still trying to do most of the work. Unfortunately, the ego cannot be controlled through the mind alone. To borrow from Albert Einstein, the problems we face due to the influence of our minds cannot be solved with the same level of thinking that created them. To put it differently, our egos alone cannot raise the frequency of our consciousness. Meditation is a critical step in the process of undoing the patterns and habits that keep us attached to the ego, clinging to negativity and lower vibrations, and keeping us in a space of self-loathing. Meditation allows us to recognize that those thoughts are an illusion. When we stop believing our thoughts and let them go, we are able to connect more deeply with our true divine nature.

MEET YOUR MIND

WITH MEDITATION, WE TURN TO OUR EGO, to the part of our mind that prevents us from being our true self, and become deeply intimate with it. Although meditation has become exceedingly popular and mainstream, it remains profoundly misunderstood. Most people incorrectly believe that when you meditate, you are supposed to stop thinking—that meditation is the *absence* of thought. As a result, many people say that it's too hard, that it can't be done because the thoughts never cease. Many people say that they want to clear their head of all thought in order to be less stressed or worried, but they abandon meditation all too quickly under the erroneous belief that they're doing it wrong or they're not good at it.

However, the purpose of meditation is not to clear one's head of thoughts. Rather, the initial stage of meditation is to watch your thoughts. One common analogy, often used by Zen Buddhists, is that thoughts are like clouds in the sky, and when you meditate, you are merely watching them pass by. Why watch your thoughts? Through meditation, you become very intimate with your own mind; you get up close and personal with all of it. By watching your thoughts, you learn not to identify with them or treat them as if they were real. Importantly, you learn not to *react* to those thoughts with words and actions that are not productive or, worse still, that you will later regret.

When you meditate, you slowly begin to create a gap between your thoughts and your consciousness. You will realize that these thoughts emanate from one part of your mind, and that there is some other part of you—the witnessing consciousness (the clear water, the Light), that is separate from those thoughts. As you begin to allow that witnessing consciousness to come forward, you can watch those thoughts as if they were pictures in a movie theatre—with ever increasing detachment. The witnessing consciousness (the part of you that watches and does not judge, but simply observes) is always watching. The part of you that is watching is also a name for your soul, for the Light in you. Meditation strengthens your awareness of that divine witnessing consciousness. As that awareness grows, your identification with the ego's incessant stream of thoughts diminishes.

By meditating, you are training your mind to consistently step out of the way, to make way for the Light to shine through. The mind can be compared to a muscle or a computer program. It requires "exercise" or needs to be "reprogrammed," whichever metaphor resonates with you. Our minds did not become what they are today without practice. We just exercised them in ways of which we were not always conscious. As discussed previously, we received ideas, notions, and beliefs from others (i.e., our parents, friends, and society) and adopted them as our own. Many of us remain unaware of what our blocks are or what patterns we keep repeating. For most of us, habitual thought patterns are rooted in experiences that can be traced to childhood. Meditation is the first step in identifying them.

We have also trained our minds to act in certain ways by watching TV, checking Facebook, playing with apps on our smartphone, texting, and emailing. In fact, many people are addicted to television, email, and the Internet. They are addicted to mental stimulation, streams of data, or constant communication. When you are out and about, notice how many people are staring at their smartphones, mindlessly reviewing texts and emails, and scanning their apps repeatedly. They will put their phones away, and then thirty seconds later, pull them out and start all over again. People are literally addicted to their devices.

The same thing happens at work: People surf the Internet constantly and look at email again and again, thinking that they are "multi-tasking." I understand the pull when the mind says that it must check email. It's just like the tug of the body that craves sugar. There is scientific evidence that the anticipation of communication via email or text creates a dopamine response, so that every time you go to look at email, your mind gives a little burst of dopamine, creating a pleasurable sensation. The Internet provides infinite possibilities for constant mental stimulation, filling your mind with thoughts and the opinions of others and allowing you to generate lots of thoughts and opinions in response. Twitter and Facebook provide a perfect outlet for the ego's desire for constant reinforcement; they allow the ego to express the random bursts of thought that it continuously generates.

Controlling the influence of the ego means operating between twin poles: between emptying yourself of the "I" (the wants, desires, repulsions, fears, limiting beliefs, and other aspects of the negative, wounded ego), and learning to truly love yourself. There seems to be a paradox here. How do you love yourself fully and unconditionally without reifying a unique sense of self, separate from others? If you empty yourself, what "self" is left to love?

The key is to recognize what you truly are and what you are not. The answer is quite simple: You are not your fears, or any other expression of emotion that is not rooted in love. This also means that, no matter how radical it may sound, you are not your personality. Much of your personality is part of your ego. The person who feels the need to be sarcastic or bitchy as a means of connecting with others, or who always deflects with humor, "tells it like it is," or "just wants to keep it real," is acting in ways that serve his or her ego. The part of your personality that reflects your true self will always be there, even if you move beyond your ego. What you find when you begin to see the ego and loosen its grip may surprise you.

How to Meditate

To REWRITE OUR DEEPLY INGRAINED programming, we must set up a new routine. The ego will resist. It will try to make you sleep in, skip meditation, and find something more "interesting" to do. Set a time and place to do it every day, even if only for five minutes. Five minutes a day every day will do a great deal more to teach the mind to step aside than one hour twice a week. It is important to acknowledge that routine does not mean *rigidity*. It is important to be disciplined and at the same time flexible.

There are many approaches to meditation; any of them can be beneficial. A very basic form of meditation is to meditate on your breath. Breathing meditation is quite simple to perform. The first step is to sit, either seated in a chair or on a meditation cushion that raises your hips off the floor, with your back relatively straight and your head resting comfortably on the top of your spine. Then either close your eyes or let your gaze soften so that you are not focused on any particular object. Once you are in this comfortable seated position, begin to focus on your breath, as you inhale and exhale. Notice how the breath feels as it fills your lungs and exits through your nostrils. When your mind drifts, simply turn your focus back to your breath.

To help focus on the breath, you can also count each inhalation and exhalation. Once you reach ten, start over. If you find yourself following your thoughts or getting caught up in a particular image, as soon as you realize that you've been distracted, return to the breathing and begin counting again, starting at one. There's no judgment and no goal. You needn't strive to get to ten, nor should you fret if you can't get past one—keep breathing and counting. Over time, your ability to not get caught up in any particular thought will grow, and you will eventually reach higher and higher numbers. Start with ten minutes a day, and then increase the time slowly. Thirty minutes to an hour of meditation each day is an ideal goal.

This is a wonderful meditation for many reasons, and chief among them is that our breath symbolizes our fundamental connection to life. We associate a baby's first breath with the beginning of life, and a dying person's last breath with the end of life. As Stephen Cope reminds us, "We all have experienced the breath as a direct link to some aspect of our inner world."[2] Indeed, there's a great deal of wisdom to be learned from our breath on how to relate to life. We can exert conscious control over our breath, deciding whether to breathe fast or slow, shallow or deep. Our bodies can also breathe without any effort on our part, so we can simply trust and let our breathing naturally take care of itself.

There are other forms of meditation that give your mind a different object to focus on besides the breath. For example, light a candle and focus on the flame. When you notice your mind drifting and getting caught up in a thought, you simply bring your attention back to the candle's flame. You can also do this type of concentration meditation without a specific object. You can simply find a fixed point on the floor, called a *drishti*, and maintain your focus there. When you realize your mind is drifting, simply bring your attention gently back to the drishti.

With meditations that require focus on something outside of us, rather than our breath, there is an added benefit. You learn to relate to objects outside of yourself in a different way; you learn to be with them, without engaging them with your thoughts. Much of our mental activity has to do with the analysis of physical objects as they enter our visual field, and concentration meditations like this type allow you to regard the physical object without immediately falling into mental analysis.

Another meditation practice is to give yourself a simple phrase or a word that you can repeat again and again to relax your mind. This is a form of *mantra* (a topic explored more at length in the next chapter). You can pick a simple one-word mantra like *om* or *love* or *peace* and then you repeat that mantra silently at brief intervals of five to ten seconds. If you find your mind wandering and pursuing thoughts that have popped into your head, simply bring your attention back to the mantra and resume repeating it internally. As with the other meditations, a mantra meditation gives your mind an object to return to when it has wandered. You are repeatedly drawing your mind away from what it wants to engage with and training it to maintain a single point of focus.

For those who grapple with anxiety, meditation can be difficult. (If you are dealing with a particularly powerful trauma or have been diagnosed with a mental illness, meditation should only be done under the guidance and supervision of a qualified therapist.) Meditation can stir up that anxiety by allowing the mind that was previously distracted (or numbed by the Internet, TV, drugs, shopping, or just constant verbalization) to be exposed suddenly to thoughts related to the events that led to the anxiety. For those individuals, if basic breathing meditation is too intense, guided meditations, which can be found on Amazon or iTunes, can help gently lead you into a meditative state. Guided meditations are wonderful for all practitioners as an alternative to the basic breathing and concentration meditations described above.

If you are new to meditation, you may be surprised at how many thoughts cross your mind, uncontrolled and involuntarily. You will soon get a glimpse of how frantically your mind works to revisit the past and predict the future. It works to stay in control according to its agenda, and create what it believes it needs to ensure your safety and security. You may also be surprised at how repetitive those thoughts are; they are often the same, or follow similar patterns. Finally, you may be surprised at how many of those same thoughts are negative. Most of us don't want to confront the fact that our minds are constantly generating one negative thought after another—usually thoughts of judgment about others and ourselves. This is the essence of the negative ego. It is a fearful and wounded part of us. Many who are new to meditation may not even realize how negative their mind has become.

Once you become aware of your negative thoughts, you can begin to keep track of how often you say or think something negative. Keep a pen and paper handy to jot down or draw a mark whenever a critical thought arises. At the end of the day, notice how many negative thoughts you've tracked. You might be astonished at how much negativity your mind is generating. However, be careful not to fuel your ego by turning that into another criticism. It is simply a measure for you to recognize the negativity that you are producing.

Once you are aware of how much negativity your mind produces, notice whether there are recognizable patterns in the thoughts. Certain themes will quickly emerge. Your thoughts are often repetitive, and they may be focused on security, the need for approval, fear of punishment, or a lack of lovability. You may also find that the ego oscillates between two poles, with thoughts of being told that you were wrong or made a mistake, coupled with thoughts of superiority in which you're telling someone else *they* are wrong. From the viewpoint of the ego, you are both victim and victimizer. The ego maintains its hold by insulting others and you, often at the same time. It is helpful to identify what the core issues are and work on them with some of the techniques presented in later chapters (and, depending on the severity of those issues, with a qualified therapist). For example, I found anger to be a recurring emotion in my life, which was related to control over situations. I would get angry when a situation did not occur in ways that I thought it should. Under that anger was a fear that if I were not in control, something could go wrong, and harm of some sort would befall me.

It has been critical to my growth to pay attention when negative parts of myself surfaced, like an angry or petulant side, or a judgmental side, or even a nasty, spiteful, and vengeful side of myself. It is important not to judge or suppress that portion of your ego, and we will revisit this topic in the final chapter. Repression merely strengthens the ego, because that part of you is wounded. To respond with judgment, anger, or resentment toward that part of you only compounds the trauma that gave rise to it in the first place. Meditation gives you the ability to see that negative emotion come up—and react to it with tenderness and equanimity. As is true of all healing, the key is to approach that part of yourself with love—the very thing that it feels it was originally denied. By learning to watch our thoughts without judgment and to love them as they go by (knowing that despite appearances, they simply are not real), we stop our efforts to fortify our fragile egos.

MEDITATION IS ONLY THE BEGINNING

THE BUDDHA'S MOMENT OF ENLIGHTENMENT under the Bodhi tree is said to have occurred after he battled *Mara*, a demon who sought to prevent the Buddha's progress. Mara sent many distractions, among them one of his daughters, Boredom. The Buddha was not dissuaded, but for many who meditate, boredom is one of the pitfalls. When you meditate, you are giving yourself a break from the mind, to enjoy the peace that comes when the chatter quiets down. Those thoughts still persist, and although you react less to them, they are still there. Meditation becomes an act of watching the same thoughts repeatedly. Over time, for many of us, meditation can become stagnant and boring, and lose its appeal.

Yet boredom can be a guidepost and not a pitfall, because it shows us where the ego still resists. Meditation alone is often not enough. Many who have been practicing it for a long time have never truly opened to the Light. They sit and meditate, but they are still operating with the same patterns and belief systems they had when they began. Anxious and frustrated, angry or depressed, they treat meditation like pushing the pause button, or putting the computer to sleep for a bit; once they get up from the meditation cushion, the programs resume. If the ego is a dark and noisy room, meditation allows us to become comfortable with sitting in the dark. Once we are at peace with the darkness of our minds, we have to take the next step and turn on the Light.

Have you ever found yourself immersed in a scene where you were watching, completely detached, but also keenly aware? You may have been sitting by a lake watching the water, or laying in the grass staring at the sky. Pause to consider that this was a form of meditation.

Do you believe that you could never meditate? Do you regard meditation as impossible, because your mind can't stop thinking? Pause to consider that the very part of you that is resisting meditation is the part of you that wants to stay in control of your mind.

If you have a meditation practice, reflect on how you view it. Is it something you undertake begrudgingly or sporadically, or is there pride or an identity forming around your practice? Do you think of yourself in a positive way because of your meditation practice?

CHAPTER 6

DEVOTION: CULTIVATING THOUGHTS OF LOVE

True devotion is not affected
by anything that happens in life.
— Swami Ramakrishnananda Puri, *Ultimate Success*

DURING THE EARLY YEARS of our life, unconditional love comes easily to us. As toddlers, we love without being aware of all the differences that potentially separate us. We love freely. We soon learn, however, to see ourselves as separate entities, and that a parent or another child can take away objects that give us pleasure; we quickly learn to love a little less easily. As we grow older, the vicissitudes of human life teach us even harder lessons in loss, rejection, and disappointment, and we adapt to those lessons by creating defense mechanisms. We form protective barriers around our heart, and unconditional love becomes much harder, if not impossible, to contemplate. Adult love comes with all sorts of conditions and strings, such as "I will love you, but only if you love me back," or "I will love you, but only if you love me the way I want you to love me."

The stern master of the ego is replete with warnings about protecting ourselves. Our minds become toxic stews of negative thoughts, and we struggle to open our hearts to others without fear of rejection or reproach. Instead, more often than not, we go on the offensive early, with sharp attacks steeped in anger and judgment. While meditation teaches us to distance ourselves from these thoughts, we can actually learn to undo the parts of ourselves that give rise to them. We can learn to undo our defense mechanisms and negative programming and replace those negative thoughts with thoughts of unconditional love. We can do this through the cultivation of *devotion*.

Devotion is the practice of spiritual commitment in which you reaffirm your belief in and love for the Divine and the life you are leading. Why is devotion an important spiritual practice? There is an unfortunate tendency in our culture to believe that when bad things happen, God is expressing displeasure, and conversely, when good things happen, God is expressing approval.

It is a fundamental misunderstanding to confuse our karma with divine judgment. The truth is that the Light does not judge or punish us. We judge, we punish, and we believe that the Light does not love us. What we experience in life is the result of our own thoughts, words, and actions. Somehow we manage to confuse our so-called negative experiences with God's wrath. We think that we are being punished, or that we are not worthy of divine love, when in fact it is we who are responsible for our lives.

The Light loves us unconditionally and always gives us what we ask for. What most of us ask for, however, is negative. Our wounded egos tell us that we are not worthy of love, happiness, and fulfillment, so we go through life filled with anger, self-loathing, fear, and hatred. Our personalities, thought patterns, and actions are built around those feelings. Almost all of our emotional strife is projected out into the world we inhabit in the form of drama, conflict, and crisis. When we put this out into the world, we draw to us the drama and conflict that we unconsciously asked for. Because we don't understand that we are drawing those situations to us through the energy of our thoughts and actions (our free will generating karma), we come to the conclusion that life is difficult, or that we don't deserve anything better, or worse yet, that God doesn't love us.

Similarly, some people only reach out to God or invoke prayer in situations where they need assistance, beseeching God to intervene in this one instance. Sometimes the request is accompanied with an apology for not really believing in God and an offer to believe if God will help out with this particular issue. Afterwards, when the situation has improved or the relief sought materializes, the person is initially quite thankful but soon forgets any sense of connection with the Divine, and resumes life as before, until the next dramatic episode leads them to turn to God again.

In other words, when we blame God for the state of our lives or turn to God only in our most painful moments, our love for the Divine is entirely conditional, based on the circumstances of our lives. We love God only when we think God loves us. This is the very definition of conditional, adult love: We only give when given to. Devotion means that we express our love for the Divine regardless of our life circumstances. When we are devoted, we believe that the Divine loves us all, equally and unconditionally, at all times. Swami Ramakrishnananda Puri makes the point, "Devotion comes when we lift the conditions on our love for the Divine."[1]

Devotion is the means by which we practice how to love unconditionally. Neutralizing the ego's negative thoughts begins with watching our thoughts in meditation. We must then begin to replace the negative thoughts instead of just observing them. We replace our negative thoughts with love—in this case, with unconditional love for that which loves us unconditionally. When we cultivate our devotion to the Light, our ego's fear-based thoughts are increasingly replaced with thoughts of unconditional love, because we are consistently aligning with the frequency of unconditional love—the frequency of the Light. Can you imagine walking around the world and looking at everyone with equal amounts of love? Having experienced it firsthand on many occasions, I can attest to the extraordinary bliss of being in a room full of strangers and feeling overwhelmed with genuine love for their wellbeing.

DARSHAN

ONE OF THE KEY WAYS TO EXPERIENCE the Light and cultivate one's devotion is to receive darshan from a Divine Avatar, like Amma, Mother Meera, or Karunamayi, or an advanced spiritual teacher, like Mirabai Devi. As discussed in the first chapter, during darshan, an Avatar transmits high-frequency energy to you. This experience often fills the person receiving darshan with the blissful energy of unconditional love. By contrast with prayer and mantra (discussed later in the chapter), darshan involves direct contact with another human being, one who embodies the spiritual truth that all of us are connected to the Light.

Darshan provides an enormous boost to your spiritual path, and is one of the most powerful ways of deepening your innate connection to the Divine. Each Avatar brings a slightly different frequency of Light, so each imparts an energy that feels different. Although it is difficult to put into words how each one feels, each Avatar's energy is consistent from one darshan to the next, as if their energy has a "signature flavor."

Whether you receive Light from an Avatar or an advanced spiritual teacher, the experience imbues the recipient with a certain amount of high-frequency energy that helps you to deepen your connection to the Light. Darshan opens the door to a higher consciousness. Although many people approach darshan with certain wishes and needs in mind, the best approach is to simply open yourself as much as possible to what may transpire. As Mother Meera emphasizes, "The energy or Light which you receive in Darshan acts in its own way. It works in its own way. There is nothing for you to do."[2]

Indeed, the transmission of Light during darshan is meant to incite a spiritual opening or awakening. For many, it is the first time they have experienced unconditional love so directly and in such a concentrated way. This is also the reason that the energy is often transmitted into the space between the eyebrows, known as the third eye, or *ajna* chakra. The third eye is the connection to your intuition and a doorway to higher states of consciousness.

Darshan is a blissful gift. Like all authentic spiritual transformation, its power can only be experienced, not understood intellectually. For some people, a single darshan may be illuminating, whereas for some others it may take many darshans for the experience to be deeply transformative. However transformative the experience may be, darshan may not be sufficient on its own to develop a sustained connection to the Light. Darshan provides the spiritual spark, but you must stoke the flame of devotion with the tools of prayer and mantra.

PRAYER

PRAYER IS A POWERFUL WAY to cultivate devotion, because when you pray, you consciously acknowledge your connection with the Light. Unfortunately, the word *prayer* comes with much baggage, and is usually associated with organized religion. Although the word can make some people feel uncomfortable, prayer is actually quite simple.

Prayer is an invocation—a request. It asks for an outcome to a situation. Traditionally, we think of prayer as asking for an outcome that we believe has not yet happened or may not exist. We ask for something we don't have to be given to us, or to safeguard something we have that we don't want to lose. Our fundamental assumption is that something needs to be changed.

Prayer actually calls forth an outcome that already exists in our consciousness but we are not yet experiencing in our physical reality. As the spiritual writer Gregg Braden has said, "Prayer is to us, what water is to the seed of a plant."[3] As an invocation, prayer is a high-vibrational request that seeks to open us to something that is already available. When we pray, our mind is not filled with its usual stream of negative thoughts; we replace our normal thoughts with something that vibrates at a higher frequency.

The power of prayer lies in the fact that when we ask for healing, we are calling forth a higher vibration of wellbeing. For example, if we are ill, we can pray for healing. We know and imagine what our bodies will feel like without pain or disease, and we are calling for that outcome, which our minds and bodies are not currently experiencing. The higher vibrations of the images and feelings that prayer invokes then attract the higher-vibrational energy of that requested state of being. The higher-vibrational energy request of a prayer attracts that outcome, until it comes into manifestation as something we experience in our lives.

Why doesn't prayer always work? Braden writes, "The power of prayer comes from the alignment between our thoughts, beliefs, and energetic frequency."[4] For example, when the underlying thought of a prayer for abundance is that "I lack" and "I am not worthy of money," or if we secretly or unconsciously believe that money is corrupting or dirty, then our request,

"Please grant me money," is not in alignment with our beliefs and emotions that "Money is dirty, and I don't feel good about having it," or "I am scared that I don't have enough." The energy of the underlying thought interferes with the prayer's request. You're emitting a lower vibration, and the Divine responds to both requests—I want money, I don't want money. (This is also why prayer has no meaningful effect when it is used merely as political rhetoric.)

This is why meditation is so fundamental, because it allows us to see what's really going on in our minds. Without that insight into what we're feeling at our core, we can pray continuously, and yet nothing will happen. Once we are aware of our underlying thoughts, beliefs, and feelings, we can effectively use prayer to eliminate the negative thoughts that have conditioned our lives.

One of the most powerful ways that prayer can be used to help erode the negativity we have accumulated is to ask for *forgiveness*. A more elaborate discussion of forgiveness as a practice appears in the next chapter, but here is a short yet powerful forgiveness prayer, offered by Howard Wills:

God, For Me, My Family And All Humanity
Throughout All Time, Past, Present, And Future
Please Help Us All Forgive Each Other
And Forgive Ourselves
Be At Peace With Each Other
And Be At Peace With Ourselves
Love Each Other And Love Ourselves
Now And Forever
Please God, Thank You God, Amen
We Love You God, Thank You For Loving Us
We Love You God, Thank You For Loving Us
We Love You God, Thank You For Loving Us
Thank You God, Amen, Amen, Amen
Thank You God, Amen.[5]

Notice how the prayer couples a request for forgiveness with devotion to the Divine. That is because the basis of forgiveness is rooted in love. We learn to experience and express unconditional love first by cultivating our devotion for the Light, and then by extending that same love to all others, who are equally connected to the Light. Using this forgiveness prayer, or any of the other prayers from Wills, on a daily basis is a powerful means of eliminating your ego's negativity.

Prayers need to be repeated on a regular basis. Why isn't a one-time prayer sufficient? The power of prayer lies in the energy of the prayer's words and your willingness to connect with the Light by uttering them. If you are attempting to remove negativity, such as judgment or anger, the energy of those prayers has to counteract the energy of all your angry or judgmental thoughts. Imagine what a daily print out of all of your thoughts would look like, both conscious and unconscious; it would run for pages and pages, and most of your thoughts would be negative. That's the cumulative energy of your current consciousness, the negative ego. When you recite a prayer, the prayer's words counteract some of the negative energy of your thoughts, replacing what would have been one more negative thought with a positive thought. You can think of them as scrubbing away the layers of negativity from your thoughts. Repeating them increases the amount of positive energy working on your behalf.

There are some essential aspects of prayer that must be kept in mind. For any prayer to be effective as a means of cultivating unconditional love and devotion, it can only be used for the highest good of everyone involved. You can pray for your wellbeing and the wellbeing of others, but you most definitely cannot pray effectively for someone else to be harmed or deprived of something. In that same vein, prayer is most effective when you surrender the results to the Divine. A prayer that defines the best outcome is less effective because you can't possibly know what is best for everyone involved. One of my favorite prayers is simply, "Light, I turn this situation over to you, for the outcome that is best for everyone involved. Please and thank you." This allows you to detach from the outcome and trust that whatever happens is the right solution.

Finally, prayer takes patience. Solutions do not always appear on the timetable in which you would like them to happen. But sincere prayers will be answered at just the right time. That has been my experience. When you truly let go, the solution to whatever situation is at hand will simply appear with perfect timing.

MANTRA

THERE IS ANOTHER PRACTICE that carries devotion in its very language—the repetition of a Sanskrit mantra. Most of us have a general view of what mantras are. We often think of them as pithy sayings that capture some message that is important to us (i.e., today I will act from my Higher Self), and that we repeat often. Those are probably more accurately called "affirmations," and they have power too, as do all statements made with sincerity. The more you repeat an affirmation, the more energy you give to that thought.

The word *mantra* here is meant to refer to particular formulations of sound that create certain vibrations. Many mantras, but not all, are in the language of Sanskrit. They often begin with the sound *om* (which in Sanskrit, denotes the primordial sound from which the universe was created) and end in either *swaha* or *namaha*, which are terms of reverence to the Divine. An example of a basic mantra for abundance (discussed in more detail later) is "Om shri maha lakshmiyei namaha." One of the foremost authorities in the West on Sanskrit mantras was Thomas Ashley-Farrand, also known by his spiritual name, Namadeva. Although the reader can consult any of his excellent books on the topic, he shared some basic principles that emerged from the Eastern traditions that are key for anyone planning to use mantras. As Namadeva explains, the word *mantra* comes from the Sanskrit words *manas* (mind) and *trai* (to set free from), which means that *mantra* is literally that which sets us free from our minds.[6]

How do mantras work? Mantras contain their own vibrations, and by uttering or silently repeating them, the mantra's frequency begins to alter the frequency of one's energy field. As Namadeva acknowledges, we contain karma (negative energy) in our energy field. The vibration of the mantra will work to remove or unblock the karma stored in your energy field.

The mantra works on the energy field of the body in two ways. First, in many cases, mantras are a direct appeal to the Light, and as such their language is of a high vibration, as is prayer. Whereas prayer makes specific requests for a certain outcome, mantras invoke a specific aspect of the Light to work on you. For example, the Lakshmi mantra, "Om shri maha lakshmiyei namaha," appeals to the aspect of the Light that offers abundance; in the Hindu pantheon, Lakshmi is the goddess of abundance. Similarly, you can appeal to the aspect of the Light that overcomes obstacles, which in the Hindu tradition is the figure of Ganesh, with the mantra, "Om gum ganapatayei namaha." When you repeat the mantra, energy is directed to some blockage in our energy field that resists whatever we're trying to accomplish, thus creating an obstacle that manifests in our external reality.

Second, mantras are continuously repeated so that the mind begins to repeat the mantra on its own; it becomes a separate thought that will, by virtue of its frequency and repetition, attempt to become manifest in this world. In this regard, mantra, like prayer, is a form of mind training that attempts to counteract our incessant negative thinking by replacing lower-vibrational thoughts with those of a higher vibration. With consistent practice, the mantra begins to repeat itself in our mind, replacing negative thoughts, particularly those negative thoughts that create the very conditions for which we have chosen the mantra.

This is a critical aspect of mantra practice because, as with prayers, when our egos are in control, we are actually already saying mantras and affirmations, we just don't realize it. Our minds are constantly repeating the same sayings over and over. Perhaps your mantras are, "I'm not worthy," "I don't deserve love," or "Things never get any better." As a result, like mantras, those thoughts grow in energy until they manifest in your life; something bad happens, which simply confirms your original thought, which leads you to repeat it. Mantra practice, like meditation and prayer, trains the mind and overrides our current thought patterns with language that is of a much higher frequency.

To begin, choose one mantra to work on a specific issue. Here is a very basic list of traditional mantras and the topics they are associated with:

Om gum ganapatayei namaha	Overcoming Obstacles
Om shri maha lakshmiyei namaha	Abundance
Om ram ramaya swaha	Healing
Om dum durgayei namaha	Protection
Om shanti om	Peace
Om aim saraswatiyei namaha	Wisdom/Creativity

The traditional mantra practice involves a forty-day practice period known as a *sadhana*. You recite a mantra 108 times, morning and night, at the same time each day for forty days; I recommend consulting any of Namadeva's books for more detailed instructions. As Namadeva is often quoted as saying, your life generally remains the same until about day thirty or so, when external events occur that try to disrupt your mantra practice, like getting a cold or waking up late. This is the result of energy in your body that does not want to budge.

Although this is the traditional discipline, and it is quite powerful, you can still derive some benefit from a mantra practice if you chant it for a certain amount of time, like ten to fifteen minutes, each morning and night. The more you chant the mantra, the more powerful its effects, as the higher-vibrational energy continues to build and works on your energy field.

Other practices can be beneficial as well. For example, on the hour, just say to yourself three times whatever mantra you have chosen. Calm yourself by breathing deeply, close your eyes, and say the mantra to yourself—either silently or out loud, whatever you feel called to do.

When doing mantras, ask yourself what it would feel like to have the area of your life you are working on to be perfectly healed. Namadeva emphasizes, and my own experience confirms, that mantra practices benefit from a strong intention, so that the energy can be directed toward an issue, even if the outcome isn't precisely what you would want or prefer. While reciting the mantra, feel and know that you are going to receive, in whatever form is for your highest good, the benefits of the mantra.

Mantras are a perfect complement to prayer because they both work on the energetic blocks in our system that are creating certain situations in our lives. For example, perhaps you are praying for a change in your financial situation. You keep asking for more money or a better job. Yet you don't appear to be having any success, and your prayers appear to go unanswered. Prayers of forgiveness will help to replace any negative energy created by thoughts of lack or scarcity with high-frequency energy. Likewise, a mantra for abundance, like the Lakshmi mantra, or a mantra to overcome obstacles, like the Ganesh mantra, will help to move the energy from unconscious thoughts and beliefs around abundance that may be undermining your prayer.

Cultivating our devotion through prayer and mantra ultimately requires that we let go of any attachment regarding the outcome. Do we truly know what is best for us? Most of us do not. Only the Light knows what is truly for our highest good. We have to relinquish expectations of how darshan, a prayer, or a mantra is going to affect our lives. For example, we may want a new job, but perhaps there is some other form of abundance that is actually more critical to our growth; the mantra will work on the aspect of abundance that we need most. That may lead to a new job and the financial abundance we seek, or something better. By relinquishing our expectations and allowing the Light to provide the solution, we water the seed of devotion in our hearts.

How do you feel about the possibility of receiving energy from another person? Does it enliven you or make you feel uncomfortable?

Pause here and consider the various ways you may have expressed devotion in the past. Have you used prayer, and if so, was it successful? Have you sought to forgive others and release anger or have your prayers been mostly material and focused on your own desires?

Have you ever used a mantra, or thought of a mantra as a form of devotion? Consider whether you might enjoy combining prayers with mantras to undo some of the negativity you have created throughout your life.

CHAPTER 7

NOURISHMENT: TREATING OUR BODIES KINDLY

Tell me what you eat, and I will tell you what you are.
— Jean Anthelme Brillat-Savarin, *Physiologie du goût*

IN *SUPER SIZE ME*, Morgan Spurlock experimented by eating nothing but super-sized McDonald's meals for thirty days. Not surprisingly, Spurlock quickly grew ill and fatigued, gained a lot of weight, and saw his cholesterol skyrocket. Even more disconcerting was that after the end of the experiment, Spurlock discovered how difficult it was for his body to recover from the ordeal. The average person does not have to undertake such drastic measures to know that most fast food is not a healthy option. The human body is an amazing gift, but many of us do not honor that gift and treat our bodies well, despite the fact that we experience joy, pleasure, and bliss in and through our bodies. As you deepen your connection with the Light and cultivate unconditional love for yourself, you will realize that this applies equally to how you treat your body.

Choices

Few spiritual books address eating as a spiritual practice, but it is essential. We must understand why we eat certain things and how what we eat matters to our wellbeing. You are indeed what you eat. However, many people do not know what they are eating, are not aware of the inferior quality of much of the food supply in America, and, even when they are informed, resist changing their eating habits.

This is true for many people who regard themselves as having a heightened sense of spiritual awareness. Part of the problem is that many of our food choices reflect physical addictions or emotional needs. We often try to eat what we don't get in other areas of our lives. Another reason is familiarity: We are conditioned to eat certain foods and not others, because that is what we were fed as children. Unfortunately, these scenarios cheat our bodies of proper nutrition.

Food is one of the ways in which we take on copious amounts of negativity and do harm to our bodies with uninformed choices. It is not my intention to provide you with nutritional guidance that is specific to your body. Most people know that they need to eat more vegetables, reduce their sugar intake, and avoid trans fats. You can consult a registered dietician or health coach about proper calories; balancing protein, fats, and carbohydrates; and detoxification. The focus here is on the quality of the food that you eat, how it is produced, and why your choices matter.

Choose organically grown food whenever possible. Buying organic means the food was produced without synthetic pesticides and herbicides. When you purchase organic food, you are contributing to the shift away from conventional industrial agriculture. Our current food system relies heavily on toxic chemicals for crop cultivation. By supporting organically grown food, you are also helping the lives of food workers who come into contact with pesticides. Eating organic is a win for you, animals, workers, and the environment.

Consuming products from animals that are humanely raised and treated is essential on a spiritual path. Most meat and dairy products come from factory farms, which means that the animals that are the source of those food products endure lives of intense pain, fear, and suffering. There is simply no reason to support an agricultural system that inflicts such pain on the pretense that we need to in order to eat. Factory farms also generate large amounts of methane, which is a significant contributor to climate change.

That same ethical concern extends to farm workers and food producers, so whenever possible, purchase certified Fair Trade products. Otherwise, the food you consume was grown, harvested, distributed, and packaged by people who may have endured terrible working conditions or weren't even paid a living wage. Your participation in that economy through your purchases, contributes (perhaps unknowingly) to the continuation of that exploitation of labor. With fair labor purchases, you honor and respect the effort others have expended to prepare your life-enhancing sustenance.

Avoid fast and processed food as much as possible. These foods contain synthetic additives and other ingredients that are not beneficial to your health. A common ingredient is high fructose corn syrup; it has become a substitute for cane sugar because it is significantly cheaper to produce. Processed foods lack the nutrients of fresh whole foods, and are intentionally addictive to keep you coming back for more.

Eating in restaurants can be a serious challenge when you care about the quality and source of your food, so you will have to exercise care in choosing meals to avoid animal products that were likely produced by factory farms, and vegetables that may have been heavily sprayed with pesticides. Luckily, many restaurants are now serving more organic and locally grown fare. Vegetarian and vegan restaurants are often, but not always, a better source for organic and high-quality food. Be vigilant and creative when looking at a menu and skip items that you know are likely derived from artificial or ethically questionable sources.

Clean, pure water should be your primary beverage. Make sure your water has been filtered so that it is free of fluoride, chlorine, heavy metals, and remnants of pharmaceutical drugs people have flushed down the drain that can often accumulate in municipal drinking water. Bottled water should be avoided, unless filtered tap water is unavailable, because it may contain high levels of contaminants from the water source or from the plastic toxins that leech into the water over a period of time. Furthermore, plastic water bottles are not a sustainable practice, using precious amounts of petroleum for a single-use item that simply ends up in a landfill or polluting the ocean. A reusable metal or glass bottle is a better choice.

It is best to minimize or eliminate soda and alcohol. Sodas are laden with sugar and artificial ingredients, particularly diet sodas, which are full of dyes and artificial sweeteners. Alcohol can be consumed in small quantities, but large amounts are obviously toxic to the body, and your liver has to work harder to detoxify the body from the effects.

BLESS YOUR MEALS

BLESSING YOUR FOOD AND DRINK is an important spiritual practice. Again, the same principle of interconnectedness applies. Someone else's labor has produced this sustenance. From nature and Mother Earth's capacity to grow, to the farmers and laborers who harvested the vegetables and raised the livestock, the workers who packaged and shipped and sold you the food, and the workers who helped bring clean drinking water to your town, someone else's hands made your nourishment possible.

Consider the number of people and the amount of energy it took to bring you whatever it is you are about to consume. When we bless our food and drink, we are expressing gratitude for all of the labor those individuals exerted to create the sustenance we are about to enjoy. Blessing also directs positive, uplifting energy toward it. By regarding our food and drink not simply as something to consume, but as a gift, we raise the energy frequency of that which we consume.

Even when we strive to eat a healthy diet, we can sometimes still make poor choices, particularly if there do not appear to be immediate negative effects. Just because you may not see immediate ill effects does not mean that you're not harming your body. Be gentle with yourself even when you do not make choices that nurture your body. Use it as an opportunity to build awareness as to why you did not make a healthier choice. You will find that when you have lapses and overindulge, there was often an emotion, such as lack of love or worthiness, underlying the decision. As Spurlock learned the hard way, it takes a lot of effort to undo the harm we inflict on ourselves with food. Instead, remember to ask yourself whether this choice is for your highest good, and then choose based on what you know your body deserves and needs, not on a craving or emotional urge. After all, the old adage is true: You are what you eat.

EXERCISE AND REST

MOST OF US DO NOT THINK OF EXERCISE as a spiritual practice, but you cannot cultivate unconditional love for yourself if you don't give your body something as essential and nourishing as exercise. The benefits of exercise are uncontestable, so much so that even as little as ten minutes of vigorous exercise a day can add years to your life. To allow disease to take root by being sedentary does not honor the sacred vessel that is your body.

Sufficient sleep is also essential. Numerous studies have documented the ill effects of sleep deprivation on the body. Many people believe that they can thrive on just a few hours of sleep, but most are deluding themselves by using stimulants, such as caffeine, to stay alert. Depriving the body of sleep is often done in order to do more work and make more money. Because our society places so much emphasis on efficiency and productivity, adequate rest is discouraged. We don't allow ourselves to rest according to our bodies' rhythms—we caffeinate rather than nap. If you have difficulty sleeping, you can implement some natural principles of sleep hygiene like using light-blocking shades and avoiding electronics for at least an hour before bed.

Standing in front of a mirror, use affirmations to thank your body for supporting you in so many ways; tell it how beautiful it is, and how much you love it. Your body performs countless processes on its own, and it deserves to be acknowledged. Many people spend a lot of time staring in the mirror pondering how their body could be "improved" or "be better looking." Practice the thought of fully accepting your body to help reverse the effects of that negativity. Self-love means you embrace your body exactly as it is in this very moment.

Pampering

PAMPER YOURSELF! Many of us do not practice enough self-love for our bodies. A pernicious and antiquated idea is that we must sacrifice as part of a spiritual path. An old mindset, rooted in scarcity, it denies all worldly pleasures as necessary for spiritual growth. While it is true that attachment to material items is linked to the ego, the Buddha taught us long ago that denial of all worldly pleasure—an ascetic life—does not lead to enlightenment. Because life is meant to be joyous, there is incredible value in activities that allow you to feel good in your body.

Nourish your body with love. Massages, restorative yoga, swimming in the ocean, pedicures, laying in the grass, and taking a warm bath are all uplifting and nourishing to your body. Many of these, such as a walk in nature or a warm bath, are not costly. For example, I find that pampering my feet is incredibly restorative because it honors the support my feet are always giving me. We often view these activities as a luxury, when studies have in fact shown them to be an essential part of restoring our minds and bodies. They are as important as eating and sleeping. These activities are healing practices because they teach us how to feel good in and about our bodies.

More than just being physically restorative and beneficial, pampering yourself embodies a key spiritual truth: It reminds you that you are worthy of receiving. It reminds you that you deserve joy, including the pleasure of feeling good physically. Many of us lack the ability to receive. Our culture imbues us with the belief that we should be independent, take care of ourselves, and not rely on others. For many of us, receiving triggers feelings that we don't deserve what we are given, that somehow we didn't earn it, which means that we are struggling with unworthiness and a lack of self-love.

In truth, we are always receiving from others; that is the very nature of our interconnectedness. Yet we deny our ability to receive. How can we expect to receive the blessings of the Light if we cannot give and receive love from ourselves? Learning to receive through the body, and feel good about it and worthy of it, teaches us to be open to the multitude of gifts that the Divine can shower upon us.

Consider your diet and food choices. Do you regard them as part of a spiritual practice? Do you think about the food you are eating as sustaining you energetically? The next time you eat a meal, think about whether the food you are consuming is enlivening you or just "filling" you.

Consider your meals as the culmination of a journey. Do you think about the people whose labor was necessary for you to eat? The next time you eat a meal, look at each of the ingredients and imagine what it took for each one to arrive at your plate. Bless and thank each person who you imagine contributed to your meal.

How often do you exercise or pamper yourself? If you don't regard it as part of your spiritual practice, consider whether you might take more walks, get massages, or do something else positive for your body.

CHAPTER 8

ACCEPTANCE: EMBRACING
EVERYTHING AS IT IS

In the state of acceptance,
there is the feeling that nothing needs to be changed.
Everything is perfect and beautiful the way it is.
— David R. Hawkins, *Letting Go*

I MAGINE THAT YOUR EMOTIONAL LIFE is like a radio dial. You can change channels just by turning the dial left or right. At the lower end of the spectrum are fear, hatred, anger, resentment, anxiety, worry, and sadness. At the upper end of the spectrum are peace, joy, comfort, happiness, pleasure, and bliss. Your daily life may feel like the radio dial is repeatedly being turned up or down, as you move from anxiety to peace, worry to relief, like an emotional yo-yo. Imagine again, that at the far upper end of the dial are some stations that perhaps you don't or aren't able to tune into very often—forgiveness, gratitude, humility, and trust. These are virtues as well as emotions that help shape your emotional outlook. Collectively, they reflect an attitude of acceptance that is present when you are connected to the Light.

Prayers and mantras can be time-consuming, but we are able to build rituals around them. These practices can be utilized in the morning or evening, or even when traveling to and from work. They require you to overcome your internal resistance (procrastination) and that can be hard for some people. But forgiveness, gratitude, humility, and trust relate to everything that's happening in your life. They provide new templates for thoughts and emotions that shape how you approach what each day brings. Can you really forgive everyone? Are you grateful for everything? Can you relinquish any sense of control that you know what's best for you and trust the Divine to lead your life? It's one thing to trust God when you're at peace sitting on a meditation cushion; it's quite another to do so with the rest of your life.

Acceptance is the station on the emotional radio dial that we all aspire to tune into on a regular basis. Acceptance is not a begrudging or resigned attitude such as, "Okay, thanks God, for this situation you dumped in my lap. I guess it'll do." When we are in a state of acceptance, we receive with an open mind and heart the present moment as it unfolds before our eyes. With acceptance, we let go of anger and resentment; we are happy for what we have and are currently experiencing; and we trust that what is coming is for our highest good. To tune into this state, we have to replace our typical mental habits with forgiveness and gratitude, out of which ultimately spring humility and trust.

Forgiveness

To forgive is quite possibly the most potent action any of us can take for ourselves and others. Yet many of us find it hard to let go of old grievances toward other people. We spend much of our emotional lives dealing with conflict with friends, family members, and coworkers. We want to feel vindicated that we were right and they were wrong—that we are the victim and they are the abuser. So we hold on to that version of events, repeating the story to ourselves (and to others) of how we were wronged by someone or a situation.

Those feelings of victimization, rooted in the past, never bring the relief we believe they will offer. Just the opposite. By refusing to forgive, we have given the person or situation that has supposedly wronged us an enormous amount of power over our lives. We dedicate so much time and energy to our resentment that we transform the other person into the powerful abuser that we accused them of being in the first place. However, we have done it to ourselves because we have *chosen* not to forgive.

Forgiveness is a choice. It may be a hard choice, but it is a choice nonetheless. Forgiveness is hard because it asks us to relinquish any resentment or anger toward another person. When we choose to let the negative emotions go, we release our attachment to our identity as someone who has been aggrieved. It feels like we have to choose to lose—to give up on any justice for ourselves because we no longer seek retribution from another person. But the attachment to our pain simply leads to more pain. When we refuse to forgive, a lot of emotional energy remains tied to the belief that the other person must be held accountable. Our conditioning wrongfully tells us that the perpetrator has to pay so that justice can be served.

To forgive requires understanding that what we perceive to be a grievance was in reality a misperception, or even a misunderstanding on our part. Perhaps someone said something mean or nasty to us, which emanated from their wounded place of lack, and we took it personally because of our own wounds; that in turn, generated unloving thoughts toward that person.

Once we understand that this individual was speaking or acting from a place of being wounded, as we were, we begin to realize that we are not different from this person. Rather than viewing each other as "right" or "wrong" (which means we are in the realm of judgment), we recognize that we are both human, with emotional wounds and patterns that cause us to act in ways that create misunderstanding and pain. When we release the resentment, empathy and compassion replace the need to balance the scales. We recognize that the person who hurt us was a victim of their ego and their own emotional wounds. With this recognition, we realize that what the person needs more than anything is compassion. We no longer view them as an abuser, but as someone who likely learned to react negatively to life's situations.

Fueled by compassion, we can also begin to take responsibility for our own emotional response and consider how we have further contributed to an already negative situation. What actions did we take that helped create the conflict? Forgiveness, then, is a gift of love toward ourselves as well as others. This releases all of the parties involved from the emotional quagmire of the past. What occurred was the conflict of two egos. Those who can forgive know its principal benefit—the feeling of relief and lightness as the energy bound up by our grievance toward another evaporates. Those who have been forgiven by others also recognize the relief that comes from knowing that another is no longer holding them responsible for some wrongdoing. When we understand that true justice lies in the gift of forgiveness, the choice to forgive becomes easy.

Forgiveness can be done in any number of ways. The easiest way is simply to say to yourself, "[Name of person], I forgive and release you completely and totally for [the grievance]." Keep repeating this statement as part of your daily practice until you begin to feel the pain of your grievance leaving you. Depending on the situation and your relationship to the person, you may feel called upon to elaborate by adding another sentence: "I love you. Please forgive me. Let us forgive each other and forgive ourselves. Thank you."

Another practice is to formulate the request for forgiveness as a prayer. A very simple yet powerful prayer can be uttered in this form: "Infinite Light, please help me and [name of person] to forgive each other and to forgive ourselves for [the grievance or situation], completely and totally, now and forever. Please, Infinite Light. Thank You, Infinite Light." You can, of course, substitute any word that resonates for you, such as *God*, *Spirit*, or *Universe*. Repeat the prayer as part of your daily practices. You can also use the forgiveness prayers offered by Howard Wills discussed in the chapter on devotion.

GRATITUDE

PERHAPS THE SINGLE MOST IMPORTANT quality that you can cultivate to open yourself more fully to the Light, and at the same time help to diminish your negativity, is gratitude. It is an overwhelmingly powerful feeling because gratitude essentially says that you have all that you need. Gratitude is the antithesis of lack. When you are not grateful for what you have, you are in a state of desire—either wanting more or wanting something else. When you are not grateful for what you have, you are saying that you don't fully recognize or accept the blessings the Divine has given you. Gratitude is inherently and fundamentally positive and uplifting, because it accepts and honors what has transpired. It focuses on the present, the here and now. It does not look to the future in the hopes of what might come. It does not review the past with regret.

One of the primary ways to cultivate gratitude is to acknowledge and be thankful for the kindness bestowed upon us by our mothers. Lorne Ladner, the author of a seminal text on psychological and Buddhist approaches to compassion, notes that many Westerners resist this notion because they feel that their mothers were not kind to them.[1] Indeed, for many people the relationship with their mother (whether biological or primary caretaker) is among the relationships cited as being the least supportive. However fraught our relationship with our mothers might be, it cannot obscure the fact that our mothers brought us into the world. Without our mothers, we would not have been gifted the enormous blessing of this life in a human body, nor would we have survived the fragility that marks the beginning of life. In fact, our relationship with our mothers should serve as a paradigm for how we relate to others. Even with relationships that have caused us enormous pain, we can always find some way in which that person has touched our lives for the better.

To change how you feel about others, acknowledge your interdependence on them. This is the lesson that our mothers teach us. As has been said many times, we are not single, isolated, autonomous beings. Rather, we are interconnected to each other in innumerable ways. When you pause to think about how the positive events and good fortune of your life have always come through connections with other people, you come to the magnificent realization that your life is the sum total of the contributions of others. As the writer Piero Ferrucci puts it, "Each brick of my house has been given by someone."[2]

Awareness of interdependence and connection to others brings gratitude for all those who have brought you those blessings. How can you not be grateful to others when you acknowledge and honor the contributions they have made to your success and wellbeing? Gratitude is the means by which you give thanks for the ways so many people have touched your life. It is one of the reasons we bless and give thanks for our food. In doing so, we honor the effort by the many people who bring us the sustenance so essential to our life.

With gratitude, our relationships with people change. They are no longer about what they can do for us or whether those connections make us better than someone else. We recognize that everyone in our life is there for a purpose, just as we have a purpose in the lives of everyone else.

Gratitude for others also helps you to deepen your compassion for humanity. We are all negotiating the joy and pain of being human. Each of us is on his or her path toward recognizing their divine nature and overcoming the negative ego. Some appear to be "farther along" and others appear to be beholden to their ego. Gratitude for another person's presence in your life, even when they are difficult and negative, helps you to see them as a blessing. They are actually providing an opportunity for you to extend love to them at a moment when they are often expressing their unconscious struggles and feeling unloved or unworthy of love. Your perspective will shift when you stop to ask yourself what has happened to this person that led them to behave this way. For example, when someone is angry, it usually means the person is masking fear or unworthiness; someone or an event has caused that person to view the world with anger. We can then feel compassion for that person's emotional state.

The value of gratitude is not limited to honoring your relationships with others. Gratitude teaches us to see the blessing in *everything* that transpires in our lives, both the "good" and the "bad." Even what we may regard as "bad" is a gift from the Divine. We often perceive events as "bad" due to our limited perspective. Countless individuals have experienced immense tragedy, only to later recognize that their lives were better off because of what they endured. Their tragedy paved the way for something else, or they learned the value of strength and persistence. Perhaps they lost their jobs and were forced to try another line of work, or maybe they suffered a health crisis and a major change in their diet enabled them to discover a new level of wellbeing.

Cultivating gratitude allows you to feel joy now, rather than waiting for the storm to break and for the blessing to be revealed. You can begin to develop faith that even when you are in the midst of a seemingly tough situation, the Divine is providing that particular experience to teach you an important lesson. It is no doubt leading you where you could not have gone without that situation. Cultivating gratitude is a beautiful practice because it instantly fosters a greater sense of wellbeing.

Set a goal of making gratitude a routine part of your spiritual practice. A simple practice is to begin your daily meditation by silently expressing everything that you are grateful for in your life, including seemingly small events that have recently occurred.

You can expand this practice by keeping a gratitude journal. I suggest starting each week off with an entry of all the people and events of the previous week for which you are grateful. Another practice is to note in your journal at the end of each day all of the people and events of that particular day that you are grateful for. The first approach, by the week, starts you out noting what you're thankful for and is a wonderful way to begin the week. The second approach, by the day, keeps you focused on the smallest events and how beautiful they are, which could be forgotten by the end of the week, if not acknowledged earlier.

Another form of gratitude I have found effective when used daily is writing a statement of gratitude on a slip of paper and placing it in a bowl or container each time you feel grateful for someone or something in your life. The result was magnificent for me after doing this every day for a year. A visual image of gratitude grows in proportion to the deepening of your emotional state as you unfold the slips of paper and review your history of gratitude for the entire year. It was an enormously powerful experience for me to review all of the things for which I was grateful, large and small.

HUMILITY

BECAUSE WE ALL HAVE SHADOWS in our personalities, we are reminded that no one is superior to or better than another person simply for pursuing a spiritual path. We all have egos. We all have family histories and karmic patterns. We all crave that profound sense of peace and fulfillment that comes from living in alignment with our souls. In short, we all want to love and to be loved.

It is important to remember this point as we experience the grace of the Light. The gratitude for the blessings that we experience must be coupled with humility. It is a trap to reproach those who don't pursue a spiritual path, or to treat others as inferior because they appear to be beholden to their egos. Humility is what reminds us that we must recognize that we cannot possibly know what someone else's path entails, and the particular lessons they are here to learn.

However, humility is not at odds with loving yourself and being grateful for your life. For some, those two positions might seem to be contradictory, as if loving yourself might lead one to think that you're unique in some way that sets you apart from others. Unconditionally loving yourself and humility are not opposed when you can celebrate and cherish yourself without thinking that you are superior. Self-love is not about protecting one's identity. As we develop unconditional love for ourselves, those aspects of ourselves that used to dictate our needs and wants begin to diminish; these were parts of our ego that demanded attention. With self-love, the illusion of our ego gives way to the truth of our soul. There is nothing more humbling than to watch pieces of yourself you once thought were important, and perhaps governed your life for significant periods of time, begin to drop off and fade away. You will realize how little of your true self you have known.

When the ego diminishes and the soul's agenda comes forward, you begin to see how humility and gratitude walk hand in hand. Gratitude is the expression of thanks for all that others have contributed to your life. Humility is the recognition that you do not have all the answers, you are not in control, and you cannot do it all alone. With humility, you embrace the fact that your soul knows the course you need to chart for your life's fullest expression. You will find that nearly all of the most wonderful experiences of life do not occur because they have been planned, but because you are led to them. Gratitude leads to humility, which leads to even more gratitude, in an endlessly replenishing cycle.

TRUST

TRUST IS THE BELIEF THAT EVERYTHING that is happening in your life is exactly as it should be. Trust is the belief that you are being supported and led, and that what is occurring for you is in perfect, divine order. You do not question what occurs, but see it as part of a larger puzzle or pathway that perhaps you don't yet fully see in its entirety. But you know that it leads to happiness.

Trust is the quality that allows you to be in the present. When you do not trust yourself or your life, you are always stuck in the past or the future. You may look ahead, riddled with anxiety about what is coming down the pike, because you fundamentally don't believe that you are supported and loved by the universe. Instead, you worry about mishaps, disease, strife, or even death. When you don't trust yourself, you look to the past, to your decisions and choices, and question them. Did I do the "right" thing?

Trust is the quality that allows your past and future to pass by and unfold without worry or anxiety. That is because trust is fundamentally a relationship of accepting—indeed, embracing—what is already in your life. When you trust, your relationships, your job, your health, and your wealth are all accepted as the perfect example of what you need right now, at this point in your life's journey.

Trust is something that is cultivated slowly, over time. You learn to trust yourself and your instincts. You begin to make choices that you no longer question, but instead, make with wonder and zeal as you see what the effects and outcomes are. You begin to see yourself as a creator in your life, building your life and world with joy and pleasure. You're not longer a passive agent, being carried along in the sea of life, fearful that you're about to enter a storm or have the boat be overturned or attacked by some sea creature. You set sail and look forward to what comes, knowing that everything that begins to enter your life is there for a purpose: to help you grow. You learn to trust that whatever happens is actually okay.

Because it is cultivated slowly, trust requires daily practice. I suggest starting with small experiments in trust. Listen to your intuition with small daily decisions in life—even something as simple as what route to take to work—and see if your intuition doesn't generally lead you to the best decision. What this teaches us is to listen closely to the guidance for a very basic decision. If I can't trust the Divine to guide me in simple matters, how am I going to trust it for major life decisions?

Trust means that there is no backseat driving with the Divine. Do you say that you trust and hand everything over, only to specify that it happen in a particular way and on a particular timeframe? This is like driving with a GPS where you put in the address, but then second-guess the GPS, don't follow its directions, and choose whatever route you decide is best. In both cases, you won't end up where you wanted to go. Trust means radical openness to possibilities that you couldn't have imagined in advance.

Gratitude and humility are the precursors to trust. Gratitude teaches you that everything that happens is a blessing, and that leads to being thankful for it. Humility teaches you that you don't have all the answers, and you don't always know what outcome is best; when you follow your heart, you don't know what the end result is going to look like. Together, they teach you that you are so profoundly worthy and loved by the Light that you can trust, fully and completely. When you are truly humble and grateful, you can't help but trust that whatever is happening is for the best, even if it doesn't appear to be so at the moment, or if the reasons are not immediately clear.

This is the matrix for allowing the Light to guide you in life: Forgive everyone, be grateful for everything, accept that you aren't entirely in control, and trust that you are loved and guided. When you do so, solutions to issues just present themselves, everything from the mundane to major life decisions, from getting into a restaurant that seemed impossible, to finding the right housing, from coming up with new writing ideas to leaving a lucrative but unfulfilling job to pursue a more heart-centered venture. Each moment of willingness to be open to a new possibility, even one that did not seem right logically, further strengthens your ability to trust the impulse to step further into the unknown.

For example, it was not easy for me to leave a lucrative salary working as an attorney to launch a holistic healing practice. Many people wondered if I had lost my mind, while others lauded my courage and genuinely wished me great success. However, leaving my job required me to accept that I did not really know what the future would hold, and to trust that the universe would show me the path. There were certainly moments of fear when I wondered if I had misunderstood the impulse, made the wrong move, or had possibly overlooked something. But those moments faded when I felt myself led in the direction I needed to take at just the right moment.

If you want to be able to tap into the guidance from the Light, all of the previous practices of meditation, prayer, and mantra work are essential for releasing negativity and limiting beliefs that get in the way of forgiveness, gratitude, humility, and trust. By doing that work, you can *accept* reality just as it is in this very moment, without any resistance. When you delegate your decisions to the Divine, you release attachment to the outcome and accept, fully and completely, everything in the present moment. By repeatedly accepting each present moment just as it is, the answers that you are seeking will present themselves without effort. Life then begins to flow, from one moment of gratitude, humility, and trust, to the next. Once you are in the flow of life, you can begin to focus less on yourself, and turn instead to another practice that is essential to opening to the Light—being of service.

Consider people that you have refused to forgive for some misunderstanding or harm that you feel was done to you. Have you wanted to forgive that person? Why haven't you? Pause here to reflect on what you think was worth holding onto by not forgiving. Can you forgive now?

Have you struggled to be grateful for what you have? Do you regard most of what's already in your life as "good enough" for now, but secretly plan or hope that the future will bring something better? Or perhaps you simply don't notice much of what occurs in your life and take it for granted, without acknowledging or appreciating it. Whatever it may be that blocks you from gratitude, try the gratitude practices outlined above for one month and see what shifts occur for you.

Do you spend much of your time worrying about the future and trying to constantly maintain control of everything in your life to avoid problems? Instead of working to avoid them, try a thought experiment: Think back to all the times in your life that you seemed to be experiencing some sort of problem or crisis, where the solution just showed up and the worst-case scenario never materialized. How often has that occurred for you? Can you begin to see a pattern where everything turns out just fine? See if that begins to create trust and therefore a new direction in your life.

CHAPTER 9

SERVICE: TAKING SELFLESS ACTION

Service is not just what you do, but what you are.
— Piero Ferrucci, *The Power of Kindness*

THERE IS A WONDERFUL SOUP KITCHEN called Mother's Kitchen, operated by a group of devotees of Amma, the divine Avatar, on the Upper West Side of Manhattan. Each month presents a beautiful scene of collective action to give to others who are in need. Gathered in the kitchen are people preparing hot vegetarian dishes, while others are chopping vegetables, slicing bread, or covering the tables with tablecloths and cutlery to prepare for the arrival of guests. At the appointed time, guests arrive and take their seats while live musicians play music, setting a festive mood. When I have participated, I have often been fortunate to have the task of helping move the food line in an orderly fashion and assisting anyone who needs help with the tray. An immense surge of love envelops me for all present. As I welcome them, I notice the gratitude in their eyes, and feel an equal amount of gratitude for having the free time and opportunity to serve them. What I experience each time I volunteer is the beauty and grace of service.

SERVING OTHERS

THE SANSKRIT WORD FOR SELFLESS SERVICE is *seva*. In sharing freely their Light with the world, Avatars like Amma and Mother Meera teach us an important spiritual lesson about the value of seva. They impart their gifts to the world without expectation of return, and yet the return on service is immeasurable. By developing our connection to the Light, we may very well feel called to perform selfless service. This is service born from unconditional love, not obligation or duty.

Serving others as a selfless act is a wonderful way to raise our frequency, and thereby work on cleansing negative karma that we have generated. We serve others because we are moved to do so. We give to others because there is joy in giving. Gratitude toward others is the seed from which service sprouts. When we feel grateful for all the ways that others have supported us, that feeling can inspire us to take action, to give back to others. Knowing how wondrous it is to feel gratitude, we can inspire that feeling in others by offering service to them. With service, we deepen our appreciation for how many people have given so much to us.

Obviously, service should not be performed because you feel obligated or because you want to be perceived by others as a good person. These are all forms of the ego that often lead to unsatisfactory results. We do not reap the benefits of service when we expect something in return, because it is no longer selfless service. Instead, we end up feeling burnt out and resentful. People who volunteer their service often begin with good intentions, wanting to give a helping hand. However, over time they often do not feel appreciated by the people on the receiving end, and so resentment builds. Thus it was never entirely selfless, as they had the hope that they would feel good about themselves by offering the service. It was done with an expectation that was not met, and the ego responds with anger and frustration.

Even if we do not always feel inspired to do selfless service, we can still work with the ego by performing service in the face of internal resistance.

In that scenario, the goal is to maintain awareness of how your ego generates thoughts like, *This isn't worth it, I've got better things to do*, or *They don't seem to appreciate this*. Use this as an opportunity to diminish the ego by observing its resistance and allowing those thoughts and feelings to come and go. Service performed in this way is still beneficial, as you are doing it for others in spite of your ego's efforts to intervene and minimize the experience. Bring your witnessing consciousness to that ego even as you perform your duties, noticing where your ego has expectations and wants to be rewarded for your service. In this way, service becomes a practice in mindfulness akin to meditation. Along the way, you are still performing a valuable service to another person by giving of yourself.

An act of service can be large or small—whether someone asks you for directions on the street or needs advice, whether you become someone's caregiver or you organize a fundraiser for a social cause. It can take the form of service we typically associate with giving, such as helping to feed the homeless or volunteering at a shelter. It can also take the form of helping any person in need. Over time, you come to recognize that every interaction with another can be an act of service.

Every act can be, in one way or another, a gift to another human being. From this perspective, your entire life becomes a form of seva.

Perhaps one of the greatest gifts that can be given is simply to embody love and compassion for those who need it most. This is not about proselytism. Rather, it is about suspending judgment of those who are still products of their karma, bound up in their egotistical patterns. By treating them with compassion, you model for them a new way of being in a world that is short on models of unconditional love and compassion. In this way, you demonstrate that listening to the ego is not the only path. In other words, you can give of your authentic self by being fully present to them. If they are open to that model, then they will begin to make the necessary changes to transform their own lives. Without preaching or criticizing, you have performed the role of a teacher, thereby giving them an enormous gift.

My recommendation is to incorporate a particular activity of service into your spiritual practices, even if it is just once a month. This could be working at a soup kitchen, tutoring or mentoring a neighbor's child, joining a community organization—anything that speaks to your interests and skills. After some time with this undertaking, you can expand the amount of service you are doing, but be vigilant as to how your ego strives to take over, turning service into an identity (e.g., you're a good person), or making it an exhausting venture (i.e., by turning it into an overwhelming obligation). As you continue along your spiritual path, you may reach the point when you no longer regard certain acts as service since your whole life and everything you do will be, in some sense, in the service of others.

SERVING THE PLANET

SERVING OTHERS DOES NOT HAVE TO BE directed at a specific individual or involve direct contact with others. The awareness that you bring to your food choices and the environment can be seen as part of selfless service: You make choices that are seemingly less convenient or more expensive because you know that they benefit others. For example, as discussed previously, you can choose to buy food that is grown organically and fairly traded so that workers are not exposed to pesticides and are paid a fair wage.

One area where we can all begin to embrace seva as a routine part of our lives, as many are already doing, is by cultivating greater awareness of our waste, specifically, what we dispose of and how we dispose of it. Many of us consume and dispose of items in ways that are environmentally unsound because it is simply more convenient to put everything in the trash. However, it is a form of service to the rest of humanity when you choose to take actions that are less convenient, such as recycling and composting. Not only do these recover precious resources, but in the process we realize how much waste we generate, which should inspire us to use fewer resources. If you use less, by definition, you waste less, which ensures the availability of resources for other people now and in the future.

Recycling and composting are both born from the same idea: Return what you've used to a form that allows it to be reused. Most of us are quite familiar with recycling: Objects made of aluminum, glass, paper, and some forms of plastic can be reused to create new forms rather than ending up in landfills. It is easy to learn what can and cannot be recycled, and to designate a separate container just for recycling.

Composting involves a similar principle in which you return organic materials such as yard waste, food scraps from fruits and vegetables, egg shells, and coffee grounds, back to the earth. The scraps are put in composting bins where worms decompose the organic material. Composting produces nutrient-rich soil that can be used for growing food or plants. By composting organic material that usually ends up in landfills, you reduce the production of methane gas, which is a major contributor to climate change.

The easiest way to go about composting is to get a small composting bin and keep it on your kitchen counter or in your freezer (which keeps it from smelling). Once a week, you can take the bin to a local farmer's market or another site that collects compostable scraps; some cities have composting pick-ups. Once you start composting, you will definitely raise your awareness of how much food you waste.

Another area in which we can all be vigilant and help to preserve the earth is by using less plastic. There is little doubt that plastic can be a useful item, but its utility aside, much of the plastic we use is environmentally unsound, particularly the proliferation of "single-use" plastic items, such as cups, cutlery, and bags. As an alternative, try reusable bags, which can be purchased at low cost and laundered as needed. Although people often say that they forget bags or that it is inconvenient to bring them with you to the store, this is simply the ego's response. Many companies make very compact bags for impromptu purchases. We did not always carry around cellphones, but people have incorporated them into their daily lives and make room to carry them everywhere. Learning to carry around a reusable bag is simply another example of overcoming a habitual practice rooted in a lack of awareness.

BEING IN COMMUNITY

A CONSISTENT THEME IN THIS BOOK is that we do not live in isolation; we are not separate from others. The same is true with respect to being a spiritual seeker and undertaking practices to become aligned with the frequency of the Light. Opening up to the Light is not an easy path in this world. Many people will feel threatened by your efforts because they are attached to their egos. To undertake these practices and to view the Light as a part of every human being also runs counter to some religious views. You may not feel that you belong in this world because you find yourself at odds with many institutions and communities. You will need to find the company and support of others who are also following a similar path. You need to belong to a *sangha* (a Buddhist term that refers to community) or a *satsang* (a Sanskrit term that refers to people who assemble to learn spiritual truths).

Enlisting a teacher helps because you will be able to connect with other students. The Avatars each have groups of devotees with whom you can connect. Mirabai has groups of Lightworkers. You can find people who support you in yoga and meditation classes, at workshops, or even retreat centers like Kripalu, Omega, or Esalen. Finding a community can also happen online, through Meetup or through online courses that include a web-based community component. There are numerous ways to forge relationships with others who are following similar paths to the Divine.

The importance of a practice community is to remind you that you are not alone in your desire to be open to the Light. Being with others allows you to deepen your practice because you bring together large numbers of people sharing a similar frequency. Being with others who walk this spiritual path gives you support as you seek to remain steadfast when those who do not support your views and practices, whether deliberately or not, attempt to steer you away from your path. In this way, being a part of a spiritual group is also a form of service, in which you give to others, and others give to you.

Being a member of a practice community is part of the evolution of a new society, one built on compassion, love, and mutual respect. When we work in community, we are able to see with full relief our deep connections with others and our interdependence on those relationships. This has been my experience as a member of a community of Lightworkers, healers, and spiritual seekers, all of whom have dedicated themselves to overcoming their negative ego, taking responsibility for their karma, and living in alignment with the Light. Being together with others, in a shared commitment to diminishing the ego and opening to the Light, helps to create a new template for human interaction and behavior. Sanghas and satsangs can provide crucibles in which to forge new types of relationships, grounded in unconditional love, rather than personal need. Our interactions with our community will show us where we are still blocked or where we still harbor limiting beliefs and a lack of self-love. It is through the shared group dynamic that we learn, through experience rather than intellectual abstraction, that we are all one. As you learn to see the

Light in all members of your community, so too will you learn to see the Light in all of humanity.

Consider the ways in which you give to others already. Some of those ways may be obvious, like taking care of your children, donating to charity, or volunteering; but others may be less noticeable. You might not even realize all the ways you give to others. Begin to shift your perspective and observe all the ways in which you already give and ways that you can give more of yourself.

Reflect on your relationship to the planet, without which life would not exist. Do you take it for granted or do you honor and respect what the earth provides? Are there ways that you can respect the planet more and serve it better? If you feel resistance around those practices, pause and reflect what that resistance might mean.

Do you feel like you belong to a community? Community need not be geographically defined, but can be a congregation of people with shared values, interests, and activities. Think about the communities you are a part of. Are you grateful to be a part of them? Do you acknowledge the ways your participation in the community benefits others, and their participation benefits you?

CHAPTER 10

REFINEMENT: LOVING OUR SHADOWS

One does not become enlightened
by imagining figures of light,
but by making the darkness conscious.
— Carl Jung, *Alchemical Studies*

IN *BEING UPRIGHT*, REB ANDERSON, a Zen Buddhist priest highly trained in meditation, recounts how he once came across a dead body in a park.[1] Rather than reporting the body to the police, he kept returning to the body and, at one point, even took a gun from the scene, which he hid in his quarters at the San Francisco Zen Center. Sometime later he was robbed at knifepoint. In response, he ran back to the Zen Center, grabbed the gun, and chased after his assailant, brandishing the weapon. Anderson quickly faced the karmic consequences of his actions, which included police arrest and outrage in his community. Perhaps the most important lesson of

Anderson's story is that his ego, in the form of repressed anger and shame, reemerged when confronted by this bodily threat.

Anderson's story is a poignant cautionary tale, one that suggests that our shadows, the wounded parts of ourselves that often cry for attention but remain ignored, can always resurface, even when we have dedicated our lives to spiritual practice. This is true even of spiritual teachers. Any teacher who tells you that they have no shadow is no longer speaking the truth; they are speaking from their ego. We all have our shadows, no matter how much we have worked to diminish our ego. Most of us have spent our lives swimming in the dark muck of life with only flashes of light to illuminate our true self. Those shadowy parts of ourselves, the genesis of childhood fears and adult missteps, continue to cloak us well after we have embraced meditative practices and offered ourselves in service to others. We have no doubt spent more time nursing our wounds and spewing venom at the world than we have in spiritual practice. This is not a condemnation of our search to escape the darkness of our egos, but a reminder of how powerful our egos can be. Our shadows have a way of hiding from the Light.

When Shadows Emerge

The shadow does not always emerge so dramatically. The shadow can come forward in any aspect of your life in which you begin to act and speak from a place of separation. The most common sign of the shadow is the belief that you are somehow superior to others. At root is judgment—a sign that you're "special" or "chosen" and have figured out something that others have not. The shadow emerges when you feel the compulsion to dictate or control others' behavior based on your newfound spiritual beliefs.

For spiritual seekers especially, because we dedicate ourselves to diminishing the ego, the shadowy parts of ourselves often go dormant, and we think they have disappeared. Your life appears to be peaceful and going smoothly, and therefore you find yourself at peace. You feel loved and in control. Time goes by, and you have not experienced any anger or fear for so long that you believe these emotions are no longer a part of you. You will soon discover that they reemerge, provoked by a seemingly external event. In fact, the anger or fear lurked in the shadow, hiding from view, unseen and ignored, until it needed to be acknowledged again. For others, the shadow might be a belief that you're not good enough. After months and months of "progress," you hit an obstacle and the old, familiar voice of your ego tells you that you're never going to get anywhere or become anything. You feel like you're standing in a quicksand of depression or suddenly deflated, like a balloon that has lost helium.

The most important step is to be gentle with yourself when you observe the ego returning. Do not convert your spiritual path into a yardstick by which to measure progress. When your ego reacts, leading to some unkind or angry thought or action, do not judge yourself. It is very easy to see yourself as regressing or taking a step backwards. You might even have thoughts about giving up altogether and throwing in the towel. Binge-watching television and eating a carton of ice cream might seem appealing after a stumble on the spiritual path. Be gentle and acknowledge those feelings. There's perfection in the sudden feeling of imperfection, because all of us have shadows. You're never alone in this regard. You have not fallen off the path. If you do judge yourself, that's okay too. Once you've gone through the steps of judging yourself, feeling bad, or even binge-eating, then stop and pick up where you left off. This is all just another opportunity to forgive yourself and to love yourself some more. Then, after the intense moment has passed, you can begin to regard your shadow's emergence, and any judgment you attach to it, as another opportunity to clear away negative energy.

The blessing is that when our shadows emerge, they remind us to be humble with regards to our spiritual development. All too often, we believe that when we are engaged in our spiritual practice, we no longer have to confront our shadows. We come to believe that we are making "progress," and the shadow disappears from our lives. That is not true. We all carry layers of karma that have accumulated over lifetimes. That is what it means to be human, after all. Even years of spiritual practice cannot entirely eradicate our shadows. Some aspects of our psyche may return repeatedly, such as addictions to food, caffeine, television, and email. It can even be addiction to righteous indignation, perhaps anger, coupled with a feeling of moral superiority, to which the ego is very attached. The key is to remain disciplined and be forgiving of any perceived "setbacks." Over time, you will come to understand that the purpose of your spiritual practices is not for you to live free from any shadow, but to enable to you to meet shadow in any place, in any form, with unconditional love.

The key to healing our shadows is to give them the love they were denied in the first place. Our shadows emerged from a lack of love, and we only tell the shadows that they are real, that the pain is deserved, by withholding love from them. You compound the pain, and relive the wound, by repressing and ignoring your shadows. This is why they persist, and why they emerge so suddenly. It is a call for love. Do not repress your shadows out of fear or shame. Instead, the only way to heal our shadows is to continue to open ourselves to the unconditional love of the Light and accept those parts of ourselves that are hidden and repressed.

It is not easy when our shadows emerge. This is why meditation is so critical. By developing a meditation practice, you will have the emotional space and fortitude to stay with your shadows' emergence and simply experience them, rather than reacting to them. When strong emotions arise, it is helpful to pause, breathe deeply, and be with them until their intensity begins to fade.

A more advanced form of this practice comes with experience and a consistent meditation practice. Once an emotion arises and you can feel it without reacting, imagine that emotion as a younger version of yourself, as a small child, or even a baby. Imagine just holding yourself, wrapped in a blanket of tender loving care. Ask yourself, what could be more comforting to that part of you that is speaking out of lack than acknowledging it with love? Tell that part of yourself that you love it completely and totally, that whatever fear it has is not real. The goal is to give that part of your psyche that is expressing this negative emotion the love that it was originally denied.

Next, ask yourself: What part of me is expressing this emotion? What part of me is feeling sad or attacked or scared? In that meditative space, an answer is often revealed, usually in the form of an image or memory from the past. It is often from childhood—one that represents a scar from an emotionally charged episode that later became a habitual emotional pattern. It's not always essential to get answers; sometimes just holding a space of love is enough. If you receive an answer from this wounded aspect of yourself, listen without judgment. Afterwards, express thanks to that part of yourself for sharing its message, and continue to hold that part of yourself in a space of love, as it has begun to heal.

As a next step, you can repeat prayers or mantras in order to help release this energy completely. You can also offer prayers of forgiveness for anyone involved in the original event that gave rise to this trauma. Finally, to deepen the healing, invoke the Light and expressly turn this part of yourself over to it for healing.

As Reb Anderson's story confirms, we all have our shadows, those parts of ourselves we have ignored and repressed. If we were to condemn Anderson for somehow failing to be a model Zen priest, we merely condemn ourselves, for our judgment is a rejection of our own shadows projected on to him. In Anderson's case, some members of his community were unwilling to forgive, but many chose compassion and forgave him, and he has acknowledged that this experience has been one of his greatest teachers. Ask yourself how you would wish to be treated if you were in a similar situation, if one of your shadows suddenly emerged so publicly. Certainly you would prefer compassion and forgiveness to judgment and rejection. So do the same with yourself. Be gentle, loving, and accepting of yourself at all times, no matter what surfaces as you examine your ego and family history.

HAVE I ARRIVED?

THIS IS NOT A CYCLE THAT ENDS. Unfortunately, there always comes a time when a spiritual seeker thinks that he or she has "arrived." "Arrival" is that place where there is nothing more to learn, nothing more to gain. Your destination is enlightenment, and you're there— your shadows have been eradicated, and your karma all cleansed. You've got the answer, and no one can convince you that this might be just a stepping stone to another path, another practice, or another teacher. The moment we think we have arrived and that there is nothing left to learn is the moment when the ego has regained control. It is the ultimate form of shadow. Therefore, we must constantly be on guard and not be blindsided.

People often think they have arrived when they have "the" answer or they speak about how they are "addicted" to spirituality. There is no single path to the Light. It is often said that all religions lead to God, and this is true to the extent that they do not teach followers to believe they are saved and others are not. There are many schools and spiritual paths; any one can be a vehicle for connecting with one's soul. Nor can we possibly know what is best for another person's spiritual path. Each person's path is meant to lead them to fulfill certain lessons and certain goals. Too many people believe that what works for them must work for everyone, and they begin telling others what they should do, instead of offering them tools and allowing them to choose. Instead of meeting someone where they are, we meet them where they think they should be. This does not mean you cannot offer advice, if asked. But many spiritual seekers, once they have learned a few practices, feel that they are now qualified to tell others what to do. This represents an astonishing lack of humility. It usually is not beneficial, because the spiritual seeker comes across as proselytizing and judgmental, instead of encouraging people to find their own way.

Similarly, when someone says they are "addicted" to spirituality, they may be expressing nothing more than genuine enthusiasm for their newly discovered path. Genuine enthusiasm is, of course, to be encouraged. But there are times when the person claiming addiction to spirituality instead means that spirituality is becoming a new identity, centered on certain spiritual teachings and practices. Quite often the spiritual addict begins to focus on teachings and practices to the exclusion of all else. This is a risk for those new to a spiritual path, because it becomes all-consuming, and they can easily fall prey to judging others who are not living up to their new definition of "spirituality." The spiritual addict may begin to associate with only those who share the same views and follow the same practices, and neglect family, friends, or their job. For these individuals, spirituality has become a means to feed the ego or avoid some trauma or pathology, and spirituality—like an abused substance—becomes the way to numb themselves to avoid feeling pain.

Addiction is not devotion to the Divine. True spirituality is not an addiction because it is not "dependence" on an external source. Spirituality recognizes that the Light truly is within you. You have no need to fashion an identity around it or focus on it at the expense of living your life. Nor do you need to separate yourself from others who don't adhere to your views on spirituality. Everyone and everything is intended to be in your life and a part of the Divine.

This is true even if you're in a toxic relationship or situation, in which people are harmful, negative, or abusive to you. If you are dealing with people who regularly cross your boundaries, try to get you to take actions that are not in alignment with your ethical compass, emotionally manipulate you, or physically abuse you, spirituality can be the tool that allows you to finally see your own value and the need to separate. This is not the same as saying that you will cast off your friends and family members because they don't want to meditate with you. In these instances of negative relationships, you are learning the need to draw healthier boundaries or remove yourself from a toxic situation. You are not leaving the relationship because the other person does not share your spiritual views; you are leaving because the person is causing you harm.

One of the key ways to distinguish between spirituality as an addiction and spirituality as an authentic practice is to look at how you relate to others. The experience of the Light is truly blissful like nothing else, but it is not addictive like a substance. It isn't a "high" that resembles something purely chemical, that you need more of to reach the same high. A drug is an artificial and temporary means of lowering your inhibitions; it does not raise your vibration, release old hurts, or heal old wounds or past traumas. Most importantly, an addictive substance does not lead you to maintain an open heart and feel connected to humanity. As you deepen your connection with the Light in an authentic manner, you learn to release your beliefs about others and to be more open and accepting. When you are open and supremely blissed out by the connection to your soul, you are encouraged to connect more with humanity, not to "disconnect" from it. Those who are "blissed out" and rejecting reality in the name of spiritual practice are, unfortunately, still feeding their egos.

REFINE YOUR FREQUENCY

THERE IS NO ARRIVAL, NO FINAL DESTINATION. Our relationship to the Light is a constant refinement of our frequency. We continually realign to the highest possible frequency available, and refrain from judging ourselves if low-vibration emotions emerge. Each time we do so on a daily basis, we return to the practice of connecting with the Light with patience and perseverance. It is as if we keep turning the radio dial, tuning into the highest frequency station we can pick up. Refinement, then, is not only accepting where we are, but also rededicating ourselves when we have become lax in performing our spiritual practices.

The first step in diminishing the ego's hold is meditation. We must first learn how our minds operate by examining what thoughts and beliefs are running like little tapes or programs over and over in our minds. Meditation allows us to step back from those inner dialogues and recognize them for what they are: wounded parts of ourselves that continue to generate negative karma. We then learn to distance ourselves from those thoughts and not react to them as if they were true. When a strong thought generates a strong emotion, we must choose to be with that emotion without responding in the way we usually would. This allows us to see how our minds generate toxic negativity that grows and eventually manifests in our lives.

With forgiveness prayers and mantras, we can begin to replace those negative thoughts with much higher vibrational language. These techniques train the mind to turn away from fear and anger and replace them with expressions of devotion and unconditional love. Shifting our negative thinking with prayers and mantras not only prevents us from continuing to generate more negative karma, but also begins to wash away the effects of the negative karma that we have accumulated.

We further develop our capacity for unconditional love through forgiveness and gratitude practices. When we learn to forgive ourselves, we no longer allow our egos to flog us for our past mistakes. When we forgive others, we no longer carry around the sludge of past grievances. With gratitude, we learn to focus on the positive in our lives, replacing thoughts of lack with thoughts of abundance. We recognize how plentiful our lives are, and we are able to express love for all that we have, rather than anger or sadness over what we believe is missing or lacking from our lives.

In time, as our connection to the Light grows, we increasingly trust in life. We come to understand that we are loved unconditionally, and that all that transpires in our lives is for our highest good. We can then let go of our efforts to control the direction of our lives and allow the Light to lead us. The accumulation of all of these practices is the state of acceptance, where we recognize that everything is perfect just as it is. We are now in alignment with the frequency of unconditional love.

Finally, we shift our focus from our thoughts and our inner world to our outer world—taking care of our bodies and being of service to others. We shift our attention from our thoughts to our actions, by nourishing our bodies properly and helping to take care of the needs of others and of the planet. In so doing, we extend unconditional love to the rest of the world.

These practices require daily effort and daily refinement of our frequency. It is hard to remain in alignment with the Light if you meditate and pray only once in a while, and spend the majority of your waking hours falling into old patterns of negativity. You cannot be a spiritual "weekend warrior" by spending many hours undertaking spiritual practices only one or two days a week.

Devote a set amount of time every day to each of these tools to develop the proper habits, and commit to your daily practice. As an initial routine, you might commit to fifteen minutes of meditation, ten minutes of prayer and mantra, and five minutes of forgiveness and gratitude practices each day, along with healthy eating and exercise; add a small good deed to the mix or make a donation as part of your seva. As your practice deepens, you can increase the amount of time devoted to meditation, prayer, mantra, forgiveness, gratitude, and service.

Many will question whether they have the time for this work. That is not the right question. Instead, ask if you have the time to love yourself and to be loved. Only you can answer that question. If your answer is yes, and you declare yourself worthy of unconditional love, the Light will make time available. Once you devote yourself to these practices, you will soon discover that the bliss of opening yourself to the Light far exceeds other activities that your ego tells you are more important.

No matter how much time you devote to your spiritual path, remember always the virtue of humility. After years of practice, your shadows, however diminished, will still be there, waiting to emerge. The process of bringing our shadows back into the Light is a life-long endeavor. Our shadows show us where we hold on to judgment and where we still feel unworthy of love. Every shadow we encounter is another opportunity to align more fully with the Light and expand our capacity for unconditional love. By loving our shadows, we come to know ourselves as the Light we truly are.

Consider an aspect of your ego that you wish were not a part of you. It may be a judgmental side, a vindictive side, a self-sabotaging part, or an anxious side of you. Whatever that aspect is, can you see where it comes from and how it tries to protect you? The next time that aspect of your ego appears, observe it and extend it love.

Do you find ways to occupy your mind, by watching television or surfing the web, so that you can avoid silence or feeling alone? The next time you feel the urge, see if you can just sit with those feelings, rather than rushing to numb them. Let your mind feel the pull to avoid those feelings and ask yourself what you're really seeking when you engage in such activities.

Pause and reflect on the ways in which you see qualities you dislike in others. Do you see those same qualities in yourself? Our shadows often appear to us through the mirrors that others provide, because we have worked so hard to ignore them. When others annoy, bother, or otherwise trigger you emotionally, consider the ways in which what is upsetting you is actually originating internally. Remember to be gentle and loving to whatever surfaces for you.

Acknowledgments

WITHOUT QUESTION the most rewarding part of writing a book is the opportunity to express gratitude to all those who have helped to make it possible. A book is always a collective endeavor, and the effort to finish one reminds us of just how deeply interconnected we all are.

My greatest thanks and immeasurable love go to Mirabai Devi, who has guided me with incredible care and love to my present state of divine bliss and transformation. Much of this book owes an enormous debt, intellectual and spiritual, to Mirabai; I remain responsible, however, for any errors or inaccuracies.

I wholeheartedly bow with the deepest devotion to the Divine Mothers—Amma, Mother Meera, and Karunamayi—for their powerful blessings and unconditional love.

Words cannot express adequately how much I love my husband, Max Goodman, who teaches me every day to open my heart even more while reveling in the immense gift of his heart.

I cannot thank enough my parents and siblings, whose support all of these years has been my touchstone. How dearly I love you all.

I am humbled and honored by my deep friendship with Will McGreal, whom I thank for his love and our many profound conversations about the nature of human consciousness.

To my fellow apprentices, Katie Loving, Drew Thomes, and Patricia Howard, and my fellow Lightworkers, too numerous to name here—thank you for walking this path with me.

Tony LeRoy, Robert Richard Wright, Paul Selig, and Kaeleya Rayne encouraged me, in ways small and large, to complete this book, and to them I offer a deep bow of gratitude.

I would like to extend a special thanks to Jami Lynn Sands, for graciously editing my first manuscript, and to Carolyn White, for her careful corrections to the final version.

It is an enormous joy to be able to express so publicly and permanently in writing my deepest gratitude to all of my teachers, from my spiritual mentors and advisers to every person whom I've encountered in my life who, unbeknownst at the time, was teaching me an important lesson. It is my heart-felt wish that their collective love and wisdom, reflected in these pages, be carried to those most in need of it.

BIBLIOGRAPHY

IT IS IMPORTANT TO RECOGNIZE that no one teacher has a monopoly on spiritual truth. Many writers have touched on the same principles. By providing a bibliography, this book acknowledges that there is a community of wisdom for you to investigate, and encourages you to explore what other authors have to say on these topics. I extend my sincere apologies to any writer who feels unfairly omitted. This is not meant to be an exhaustive survey or a comprehensive bibliography; only those works that contributed to this book have been listed.

Anderson, Reb. *Being Upright: Zen Meditation and the Bodhisattva Precepts*. Berkeley: Rodmell Press, 2001.

Ashley-Farrand, Thomas. *Chakra Mantras: Liberate Your Spiritual Genius Through Chanting*. San Francisco: Red Wheel/Weiser, 2006.

———. *Healing Mantras: Using Sound Affirmations for Personal Power, Creativity, and Healing*. New York: Ballantine Books, 1999.

Bayda, Ezra. *Zen Heart: Simple Advice for Living with Mindfulness and Compassion*. Boston: Shambala, 2008.

Braden, Gregg. *The Isaiah Effect: Decoding the Lost Science of Prayer and Prophecy*. New York: Three Rivers, 2000.

Cope, Stephen. *Yoga and the Quest for the True Self*. New York: Bantam Books, 1999.

Devi, Mirabai. *Samadhi: Essence of the Divine*. Encinitas, CA: Mirabai Devi Foundation, 2010.

Ferrucci, Piero. *The Power of Kindness: The Unexpected Benefits of Leading a Compassionate Life*. New York: Tarcher, 2007.

Fischer, Norman. *Taking Our Places: The Buddhist Path to Truly Growing Up*. New York: HarperCollins, 2003.

Harra, Carmen. *Wholeliness: Embracing the Sacred Unity that Heals Our World*. Carlsbad, CA: Hay House, 2011.

Hawkins, David. R. *Letting Go: The Pathway to Surrender*. Carlsbad, CA: Hay House, 2012.

Jung, C.G. *Alchemical Studies*. Princeton, NJ: Princeton University Press, 1983.

Ladner, Lorne. *The Lost Art of Compassion: Discovering the Practice of Happiness in the Meeting of Buddhism and Psychology*. Epub ed. Sydney, Australia: HarperCollins, 2007.

Linville, William. *Living in a Body on a Planet: Your Divine Abilities*. N.p.: William Linville, 2011.

Mother Meera. *Answers, Part I*. Dornburg-Thalheim, Germany: Mother Meera, 2008.

———. *Answers, Part II*. Dornburg-Thalheim, Germany: Mother Meera, 2008.

Puri, Swami Ramakrishnananda. *Ultimate Success: Discourses on Spirituality*. San Ramon, CA: Mata Amritanandamayi Center, 2004.

Nepo, Mark. *The Book of Awakening: Having the Life You Want By Being Present to the Life You Have*. York Beach, ME: Conari, 2000.

Schucman, Helen. *A Course in Miracles*. Mill Valley, CA: Foundation for Inner Peace, 2007.

Selig, Paul. *The Book of Love and Creation: A Channeled Text*. New York: Tarcher, 2012.

———. *I Am the Word: A Guide to the Consciousness of Man's Self in a Transitioning Time*. New York:

Tarcher, 2010.

Tolle, Eckhart. *A New Earth: Awakening to Your Life's Purpose.* New York: Penguin, 2008.

———. *The Power of Now: A Guide to Spiritual Enlightenment.* Novato, CA: New World Library, 2004.

Walsch, Neale Donald. *The Complete Conversations with God: An Uncommon Dialogue.* New York: Putnam, 2005.

Notes

Chapter 1
[1] Mother Meera, *Answers, Part I*, 74.

Chapter 3
[1] Walsch, *The Complete Conversations with God*, 20.
[2] Bayda, *Zen Heart*, 46.
[3] Nepo, *The Book of Awakening*, 309.

Chapter 4
[1] Schucman, *A Course in Miracles*, 23.
[2] Harra, *Wholeliness*, 1.

Chapter 5
[1] Bayda, *Zen Heart*, 54.
[2] Cope, *Yoga and the Quest for the True Self*, 206.

Chapter 6
[1] Puri, *Ultimate Success*, 185-86, 194.

[2] Mother Meera, *Answers, Part II*, 40.

[3] Braden, *The Isaiah Effect*, 181.

[4] Ibid., 188-89.

[5] Mirabai Devi emphasizes the importance of using forgiveness prayers in spiritual practice. For additional prayers, consult Howard Wills' website, www.howardwills.com/prayers.

[6] Ashley-Farrand, *Chakra Mantras*, 39.

Chapter 8

[1] Ladner, *The Lost Art of Compassion*, 181-82.

[2] Ferrucci, *The Power of Kindness*, 234.

Chapter 10

[1] Anderson, *Being Upright*, 186-88.

About the Author

Patrick Paul Garlinger first experienced the grace of awakening many years ago when he began to meet numerous spiritual teachers and experience higher states of consciousness. While training under the renowned spiritual teacher, Mirabai Devi, Patrick underwent a profound evolution of his inner world. As his ego began to dissolve, he began to see different frequencies of Light. This radical transformation led to a kundalini awakening that opened his intuitive faculties, and he began to channel works of spiritual wisdom, setting him on a radical new path. Previously a professor of Spanish literature and an attorney, Patrick is now a spiritual writer who provides intuitive guidance and healing services to individual clients. He lives in New York City with his husband and two cats. For more information about his writings and services, please visit www.patrickpaulgarlinger.com.

CPSIA information can be obtained
at www.ICGtesting.com
Printed in the USA
LVOW08s1522060617
537124LV00003B/603/P